# LIGHT UP THE WORLD

# LIGHT UP THE WORLD
Inspiration for a New Humanity

## MARK SIMPSON

Published by Mark Simpson
www.marksimpsonbooks.com

Copyright © Mark Simpson, 2019

First published, August 2019

ISBN: 978-0-6485781-1-6

A catalogue record for this book is available from the National Library of Australia.

Book and cover design by Liam Relph.

*For my open-hearted wide-eyed girl*

## BEGIN ANEW

The end a new beginning it depends on how you see
the start of us the end of them, new ways for all to be
All the words from start to end from below to above
are here to take you back again to know yourself as love

So see yourself on every page in every breath you take
In every smile and every tear, each insight that you make
As you read through this journey the one who watches on
is love that's deep inside of you and with you all along

Find endings or beginnings there are both and neither here
The first step is to be yourself, for love to reappear
Know no end is there for you on this book's final page
Just kind and wise beginnings, true love's new dawning age

# CONTENTS

Awake, 3

Follow Your Heart, 15

Moving On, 25

Courage, 37

Silence, 47

Darkness, 65

Rising, 81

Soul, 125

Creativity, 145

True Nature, 149

Inspiration, 163

Light Up the World, 177

Love and Beyond, 227

# FOREWORD

*Light Up the World* is a delicately woven narrative of life, love, loss and the redemptive power of the human spirit to realise its unlimited potential.

Its author, Mark Simpson, is a gifted writer, poet, yoga teacher and a true visionary leader of our times.

In the years I have known Mark, he has been both an esteemed colleague and treasured friend. I remember meeting Mark for the first time, and what struck me the most was his calming, loving presence. Little did I know then, that one day I would have the honour of writing this foreword for his wonderful book.

Mark is an ancient soul, gentle and wise; he lights up the world with his strength of spirit which is kind, heartfelt, commanding and compassionate.

As you journey through the pages of this book, you'll uncover timeless wisdom that is soulfully stirring, deeply provocative, and written with more than a touch of candour.

According to many of the world's great spiritual traditions, creativity opens the doorway to self-realisation. In *Light Up the World*, Mark's words inspire the mind, touch the heart and soothe the soul. Their style and presence are far-reaching and will move you with their heartfelt intentionality. What you read in the following pages you can trust to guide you back to wholeness again.

Mark's greatest gift in *Light Up the World* is his ability to create a bridge of understanding between the dark and light, the past and future, the body and spirit. He shows us that the depths of our psyche are rich with the eternal promise of new life.

His message is pure and simple: The transcendent power of love heals ourselves and the world.

It was our beloved Rumi who said, "I looked in temples, churches and mosques. But I found the divine within my heart." Mark's language is a living model of divinely inspired creativity. It awakens courage and the extraordinary possibilities that dwell within. It explores the realms of the imagination, describing with searing honesty, that it is in the darkness before dawn that our inner light, like the sun, will rise to a new day.

Each chapter is a delight – overflowing with insight, compassion and awareness. It is music for the soul and an enduring treasure, sending out a clarion call to guide us home to live the life we are destined to live.

*Light Up the World* invites us to embrace our true nature and trust the unfolding journey of our soul. When we do this, something magical happens – we discover ourselves anew and become a force for good in the world.

My wish is that Mark's books, workshops, classes and overall sphere of influence will speak to your heart and the hearts of millions of people all over the world.

Thank you, Mark, for creating such a beautiful and inspiring book. Its brilliance sends out a message of hope and lights the way for a brighter future for all of humanity.

Makita Gabriel

Founder of 'The Soul Vida Method'
Author of *Soul Vida – Body, Breath and Soul*
Perth, Western Australia.
www.soulvidafit.com.au

# PREFACE

This book is an invitation to inspire new ways of being in ourselves and in the world. It points to the truth of who we are and explores what that means for us individually and for humanity. It is an opportunity to look within for our own truth, not just superficially, but to look deeply and uncover our essential nature.

While it is an account of my own journey of coming to understanding, it is also a reflection on a path to wholeness and a greater possibility of unity for all of us. I wrote these words over three years of great personal change and self-inquiry, though they reflect a more extensive and larger process of transformation that is available to everyone. Just like each of us, this work has been a lifetime in the making.

As with our own being, so too these words hold the seeds of potential of everything we need to realise the ever-present truth of who we are, and to support awakening for all. The fruits are greater presence, awareness, authenticity and compassion. We can share these freely to create a more kind, peaceful, equitable and sustainable world.

It is an offer to inquire and reflect – to find stillness and discover your own essence. Hopefully you will be inspired and encouraged to uncover, grow and share a sense of your own inner divinity with others.

Ultimately, it is a book about personal and collective truth, empowerment, wisdom, and waking up to our true nature and our greatest potentials. It contains insight and support for the work of transforming ourselves and the world, and to encourage greater harmony, peace and understanding.

Most of all it is written with love. It is for all beings.

~
AWAKE

## ONE DAY

One day I saw myself as love
No hell below no heaven above
In just one look I saw it all
The empire of the ego's fall

I always knew there was something deeper inside me.

A feeling I was much more than I thought, and that there was more to the human experience than we are taught to believe. More than our consensus reality that tells us we are just a body and a mind; that we should live our life in a certain way and within the parameters of what convention and conditioning tells us.

One day that deeper knowing woke up in me. A direct experience that I was a lot more than my mind, my body or even my sense of self. Everything that had gone before was done and in a moment reduced to a broken empire whose days were numbered. Though just a flash, it was so sudden, so bright and revelatory that I knew to my deepest core that life would never be the same again. My mind had no frame of reference for the experience, but it was a glimpse past ordinary reality into my true nature.

My entire sense of self was undone. How I functioned in the world, how I related to myself and others, all of it changed, not immediately but steadily, yet in some ways dramatically. The experience started me on a deeper journey into the nature of reality, of self-inquiry and a process that called into question every aspect of my being. It felt as if I were being asked to look deeper and further, and to understand more. More about what I already knew in my heart existed deep within me. On every level: physically, mentally, emotionally and spiritually, I was being asked to open up, and while the changes were taking place inside of me, they inevitably led to big life changes on the outside.

A steady undoing of my old self began and a simultaneous reforming and restructuring was underway. There was a purging of the old sense of self as old patterns came up for examination and were let go. There was nothing the process didn't touch or call up, including a great amount of subconscious material. At every level – body, spirit and mind – things changed and started to move. I didn't even know who I was some days. Amongst it all was a wonderful recognition of what I am and what I am able to give at the deepest levels of my being.

My experience is not unique. Consciousness is waking up in people everywhere and it has consequences not just for ourselves, but for our humanity. If we recognise the unity of all existence, there are ways of being, understandings and patterns of behaviour that are unavoidable. There are values, beliefs, traits and qualities that emerge and establish themselves in us. They are both the cause of the work, the means of doing the work, and the work itself. They are what we can grow inside ourselves and what we can bring to all aspects of our experience, including our relationships with ourselves and others.

This is the journey we are all on. Whether we understand it yet or not. At a deeper level this is the journey of all of us – the discovery of our true nature.

It is an invitation to wake up to the truth of who we are and the universal truth of consciousness itself. 'The empire of the ego' is everything our mind thinks we are. The sufferance, the fear, the stories, the unhelpful habits and patterns that exist within us: both individually and collectively. By becoming more conscious, we can step into a new understanding of the body-spirit-mind connection and take it further still. We can nurture a deeper interrelationship with others, with our communities, with the environment, and with all beings. A connection and way of being in the world that is as strong and powerful as it is kind and compassionate.

We are waking up to a different way of being that has the capacity to change the world, and to meet and deal with the individual and collective problems we face. The call to wake up is a latent possibility in all of us. All of us have the seeds of potential, though not all of us have the inclination, circumstances or determination to turn our attention towards the realisation of that potential. This is not a new process – humans have known this ability for thousands of years. It has formed the foundation of both shamanic practice, and indigenous wisdom; all religions and spiritual traditions point towards the same realisation.

This book is a personal journey, and it is also a continuing journey. Many wise and helpful teachers have helped me to realise the underlying truths of my experience and understanding. Each of us has our own journey and path to walk, but there are common truths and ancient wisdom that support us as we go, if we stop and care to listen. At the same time this book is an invitation to embark and reflect on a universal journey from separation to integration.

It is the wise, compassionate teachers of many traditions who help lead us towards the deepest truth, and it is their wisdom that the world is urgently in need of. Wisdom that can return us to balance and wholeness to love and kindness.

The process and the gifts are universal. The birthright of every human being.

Waking up is love in action. It is for everyone.

## BEAUTY ON THE BEACH

I saw beauty on the beach
So close at hand so out of reach
So divine so barely shown
So vivid real but so unknown

Something timeless about the look
So I read in wisdom books
So here and now so still a dream
So gone again and so unseen

The divine in each of us can feel like it comes and goes.

On one level, it does. The transient flow of life and our lived experience can pull us in many directions. Through it all we touch our own greatness at times. To live in it is a practice.

Most of us are walking around with our divinity hidden from view, concealed from others and often especially from ourselves. Buried under layers of demands and expectations, we frequently don't even know the truth of who we are at our most authentic. Uncovering our personal truth and essence is a wonderful journey.

If we look deeply, we can see beauty and greatness in others. Their highest self and their essential nature. The most loving, compassionate and kind version of another, replete with their creative talents and quality of heart. To be able to see these qualities in others takes effort and a willingness to put aside both the judgements our minds make and the labels we learn to attach.

Sometimes we encounter others who are an embodied expression of their highest truth. Such an encounter can be so fleeting, yet leave such a profound impression, we might be forgiven for doubting how real the experience truly is. Yet it is undeniable. We feel it in our hearts.

Divinity is ever present if we would only allow ourselves to rest more fully into it. This is the timeless divinity, which can arrive in one look, one shared moment, a flash of deep insight. Our true nature. This is the truth our wisdom traditions point to. It is so real yet our minds don't know it nor can they comprehend it.

Real beauty is in and around us all the time if we only learn to see it. Our sense of personal divinity may come and go, but hopefully we learn to grow and sustain it.

The truth of who we are is always here.

## WHILE I WAS SLEEPING

While I was sleeping a beautiful soul
planted a seed that started to grow
Bathed in the sunshine
battered by storms
Tempered by cold
nurtured by warmth
Watered with kindness
more seeds still to sow
Awakened a love
that time doesn't know

There are beautiful beings in the world who point us back to ourselves. Who we truly are. They are the constant gardeners of humanity.

They are of all faiths and traditions, though many do not identify with any. So too, many faiths and traditions have teachers and followers who do not adhere to the essence of those traditions. In some cases there can be a complete distortion of an ethos into its extreme opposite, where positions of power and influence are used to subjugate, intimidate and abuse others. This has happened historically in the collective and continues today in many guises, but such distortions deny the compassion, kindness and respect for humanity that lie at the heart of those traditions.

I have been very lucky to encounter and learn from some wonderful teachers. They are an inspiration for the continuing journey. They don't belong to any one faith, but I have found them in Buddhist, Yogic, Indigenous and Shamanic traditions, and even in the most unlikely places of daily life. There are great teachers and beings present in all traditions and cultures. They can be hiding in plain sight as those who steadily use their positions of influence for the greater good of humanity and the planet. They are also the beautiful and compassionate teachers, therapists, carers and workers, committed to our health and wellbeing. They are the wise elders and wisdom keepers.

Great love and compassion can be very powerful, even in quiet settings. Their loving hearts and powerful essence radiates. Being in their presence is enough to remind you who and what you really are. Truly great teachers are an embodiment of their teaching. Their words have power, their physical presence is a reflection of their understanding and their lives are an example.

Their supply of seeds is endless for having cultivated them within they are free to give more fully of what they have to others. They know what nutrients and tools they need and can generate and share them wisely too.

~

FOLLOW YOUR HEART

## QUIET VOICES

The voices that I sometimes hear
are wonderful because they steer
me in the way that I should go
when I am quiet and softly know
that in my heart I've always known
the things that are now being shown
an open door to what's behind
the new world that we're still to find

We all know our deeper essence before the rigid structures of the ego are laid down and obscure it from us. We can see it in babies and the young who are so alive and curious. They engage with the world through feeling and perceiving on a much more subtle level than we soon become accustomed to. The conditioning of our formative years often closes off aspects of who we are and our more subtle awareness.

As we undo the loud commentary of our minds and the internalised voices of our conditioning, so we can relearn a different and more original way of perceiving.

There is a power within us that is our own individual life force, our unique expression of who we are. We can access this deep knowing by listening more fully to our hearts. The heart voice is soft and quiet, but it is strong and true. Allied with a powerful intellect, it can become a force for good and profound change in both our inner and outer world.

There are even the voices of other realms that if we are quiet enough to stop and listen we might hear. When our mind is quiet and allowed to settle, we open up more and more.

We hear our heart in stillness.

## LISTEN TO THE WISDOM OF YOUR HEART

Listen to the wisdom of your heart
The sound which comes before the thought
Breathe before you start to think
Clearest sight before the blink

We tend to know intuitively what we need or want. Our heart knows and our body's own natural intelligence knows. Being able to act from that place of innate knowing can become spontaneous, but it takes practice.

If we ask ourselves a question when we are quiet and centred, and listen to the first thing that comes to us, our answers will arrive quickly and accurately. This is the seat of our intuition and creativity – our heart's knowing. It includes both the seeds of who we are and what we are longing to do, as well as the guidance and trust we need to lead us towards that greater expression of ourselves. It is so fast and accurate that our mind can end up talking us out of it.

In the same way, accessing a deeper sense of calm and quiet in ourselves helps us to make better decisions. By calming ourselves we are able to find a deeply loving and compassionate space within which allows us to meet the difficult moments of our lives with greater truth and clarity. Choosing and making decisions under stress, or in the presence of out-of-control and overly-strong emotions isn't helpful. That is not to say that emotions themselves aren't natural and don't weigh in the balance in making decisions, but they are the signposts and indicators for what we know and want at a much deeper level.

My mind loves to ruminate. It has a momentum of its own that can get out of control. Second guessing, doubting and fearing. It has many dialogues and if I think too much about the number of hours, days, months and years I have spent in those thought patterns, I can go to a very dark place. Ruminating about ruminating, fear of fears, doubts about doubts. It is a vicious circle. It feeds on the thousands of opportunities for distraction, the internalised voices of others, and the desires of others to reach into your being to tell you: you are not enough, you should be doing something else, you should be buying their products or giving your attention to the latest fleeting attraction.

Coming back to ourselves, by focussing on our breath and being able to calm our body and mind, helps lead us to a more constructive space where we can access our deeper knowing – even when we are considering the most difficult decisions we can be asked to make as humans. It can make our day-to-day lives more peaceful and joyful too.

## TRUST YOUR HEART

Trust your heart when all around
the voice of doubt the only sound
Its silence speaks inside of you
Timeless, wise, forever true

Voices of doubt come from within and from without. Stepping away from consensus ideas of what is right and wrong to follow our heart and own deeper knowing can be confronting to others. Especially to those who know us as we have always been, or more accurately, how they have always perceived us to be. It is us continuing to play the game of 'I will be what you want me to be, or expect me to be' that keeps us stuck in loops where we struggle to break free of our mind and step into our deepest sense of self and our dreams.

Deeper still is a knowing that is greater than all the mind chatter and even the new stories that are laid down. It is a growing sense of trust in a deeper process unfolding. A process of opening to our fullness, our essence and beyond. It is the capacity to enter into the state of silent stillness where we access the quiet, knowing voice in us that tells us everything is exactly as it needs to be; to trust that we are following something much deeper and more true than we can rely on our mind to tell us.

The heart's knowing is so great. We don't access it through our mind. We know it deeply. Its wisdom is far beyond what our conscious mind thinks.

~

MOVING ON

## MOVING ON

I'm moving on to other things
For in my heart a songbird sings
So this goodbye is harder still
For it knows love and bears no ill

We make choices that serve our highest good and potential with love.

There may be a point at which we recognise that the life situation we find ourselves in is not supporting our deepest truth or our highest self. It can be a difficult time as we feel the increasing tension between contentedness and the urge to grow into our fullness.

For me, there was a recognition that an amazing relationship and setting that was full of love, respect and wonderful experiences was not supporting me. Half a lifetime of achievement in a conventional sense: a beautiful partner, a beautiful home, a well-paid steady job in the corporate world. A recognition that though it had been a wonderful journey, it was not sustaining the innermost essence of who I am. The part I really knew had always been there underneath, in training and waiting to flourish. My truth.

To leave the love I knew for my heart's knowing felt like an impossible decision for a long time. In the end I knew I had to trust myself as difficult as it was, and would be. It is one of the hardest things I've ever done.

Choices that ask you to choose to hurt someone you love or yourself cut all the way down. They can feel like they are breaking you. It shattered me for a while.

Decisions that go to the deepest part of our heart or being are the hardest. There is no easy way except with kindness and compassion, for others and for ourselves.

We know in our heart if our soul's purpose is being fulfilled.

## SOMEWHERE

Somewhere down this sun-drenched coast
sits the girl I love the most
Who wonders what has happened to
the happy days, the *I Love You*'s

We both sit down and gaze upon
the same ocean and setting sun
No longer sitting side by side
A growing love that couldn't hide

I gave my life to you
My breath, my love, my heart to you
And I nearly died for you
But my soul can never lie for you

These fears are of a world so dark
These tears are of a broken heart
These eyes that cry at every sign
that I was yours and you were mine

Sometimes we give ourselves so completely to others that we lose sight of who we really are. All the things we share with another person are beautiful, they are part of the magic of life.

Heartbreak is heartbreak. There is no avoiding it. It hurts. When we grieve for lost love or the loss of another, every sign, reminder, song or shared memory can be both beautiful and simultaneously heart-wrenching. It is a painful paradox.

Ultimately though, soul decisions are made deep in our hearts and the rest is for us to work out as consciously as possible. Being with the pain fully and not overindulging it would have been an easier way for me to deal with it but really – when it hurts, it hurts.

The greater the love, the greater the grief.

## CALLING TIME

How on earth to move on from here?
when all I see is endless fear
when everything I've ever known
is all undone and long outgrown

How to move on when the feeling is gone?
when the brightest star has been outshone
and nothing's left when time is called
and love for one becomes love in all

Growing asks us to face and move through our deepest fears.

The thought that I had put so much of myself into my brightest star and that something far greater had somehow eclipsed it was disorientating. I had outgrown an old sense of self and how I functioned in the world. At the same time, values and belief systems that served an old way of being and relating were changing. I also realised how many past decisions I had made out of fear. Fear of not fitting in, fear of hurting others, fear of failing, fear of being myself. What I had strived for for so long was not in itself sustaining, and at the same time I felt a call to step further into life itself, and to inquire into who and what I really was.

To step into our fullness or take a path of heart and spirit is an open invitation. Sometimes we don't choose the invitation and some of us don't seek it. If it comes, it doesn't matter what it changes in the process, it comes. All of it.

A new set of fears came in. 'How will I survive?' 'What am I going to do?' The material world felt increasingly empty with its distorted values, histories and ways of being that were so far out of alignment with more universal truths.

Ultimately we arrive at our learning and a deeper understanding, which in itself opens up new possibilities. 'How will this insight help me and others?', becomes a dominant question and new motivation for life.

What is our deepest truth? How can we live from that and how can we use it to benefit others?

## THE HEART IS TRUE

In the end I knew I had to set my spirit free
to love again with all my heart the deepest part of me
The hardest part is knowing a love I've hurt so much
a kind and loving being whose soul I couldn't touch
I look around into the eyes of blank confounded faces
who cannot reconcile that we'd end up in different places
Confusion that I know is just a pattern in my mind
is stronger in the face of growing love it cannot find
For in my heart the answer waits to questions that arise
The heart is true and never fails the mind tells only lies

In a society ruled by heads and conventions, heart-based decisions can look out of place. We glorify many ideas and stories that are not based on truth. Many of them are distorted and unhealthy. Notions of a successful or meaningful life are often wrapped up in material wealth, status and appearances. In the face of those dominant concepts and accepted practices, following our heart can seem incomprehensible.

The mind tries to bargain with the heart for all it is worth. It gets very confused. It can set up an inner storm that seems impossible to navigate.

For me, there was a time when I seriously thought I was losing my mind. The look of judgement in the eyes of others who did not and could not possibly understand were difficult to bear, and it played havoc with my ego which was striving for conformity, acceptance and recognition. All the time I felt a desperate feeling of wanting to be seen for who I truly am. My most authentic self underneath all the small talk and superficial appearances.

Standing by those heart decisions in the face of expectations and the judgements and responses of others is tough. Their words echo in our head and add to the voices of doubt and confusion in our own mind. Learning to make heart-based choices and staying with them is a doorway to intuition, truth, authenticity and life lived deeply.

The mind doubts, the heart just knows.

## A SONGBIRD

You were my dream and now the dream has gone
A songbird left without a song
Empty days an empty heart
An end to ends a time to start
To wonder what the new will bring
And give my voice a song to sing

When a dream dies there is the holding on. To the wonder of it, to honour it, to love it, to try and get it back, even holding on to the pain of losing it.

Ultimately there is an end to endings. Before the new arrives there is the blank page on which the future will be written. Full of potential. New dreams to dream and new realities to create. Inner and outer.

A songbird cannot stay silent forever.

~

COURAGE

## SURRENDER TO THE UNKNOWABLE

My heart is breaking
Not just breaking apart
but breaking open
that the broken is dying
that the unbreakable is being shown
that in leaving what I know
I may know everything
that in knowing everything
I know nothing
and surrender to the unknowable

As the heart opens we come to realise more of ourselves, more of our shared human existence and more of our true nature. We find our kindness and compassion.

My heart has been breaking open for years.

I had to make the hardest choice of my life to break the heart of another beautiful person, my best friend and life partner, for my own deeper needs. It broke my heart a thousand ways.

I'm easily touched by beauty, acts of love and kindness – great and small. I have sobbed my heart out in the presence of nature's wonders; at acts of unconditional love; at the words of great poets; the wisdom of kind teachers; the works of great artists; the suffering of humanity. At promises made and broken; at self-love that I had denied myself for years; at the ability of humans to persevere and care for others in seemingly unbearable adversity.

The broken parts of me that were dying were either so loud they destroyed me, or were parts that I ran away from. It is not that the broken truly dies. In some way it does, but really it goes into hiding in plain sight. I know those broken pieces are there, I know them intimately and at times they can be a cause of unnecessary suffering, but they run the show less and less. I try and relate to them more usefully. The wounds are healed and I try not to break them open any more.

As well as the broken, there are parts of us that are unbreakable. They will withstand anything, anyone or any situation. The human spirit, our life force itself – is capable of extraordinary feats. The capacity to have goodwill towards others. To recognise our shared basic human needs for shelter, food, water and love. Even in the hardest hearts and on the darkest days there is hope and the potential for goodness.

Deeper still is the opportunity to open to the truth of who we really are. Ultimately unbreakable and indestructible, as souls and beyond even the idea of souls.

The mind that thinks it knows everything, knows little of the truth. It keeps us enthralled with endless games happily helped along by internal voices and external distractions. Even the great minds and philosophers have long recognised that there are limits to cognition, that we cannot solve our problems without further exploration into the nature of consciousness and reality. True insight and genius are beyond mind.

Even when we realise some degree of truth, or experience consciousness in any of its transcendent forms, there is always something greater. We shift to a different kind of knowing that is not of the mind. The mind will still come along, but more as a servant than a master. Experience and integration are part of growing and opening our hearts.

Beyond that we might touch the infinite, but we can never truly know it.

We surrender to the unknowable.

## ALWAYS HERE

Love in all its varied forms
keeps me dry in winter storms
Holds me in its gentle arms
lights my day and keeps me warm
Holds my hand when I get scared
listens when my soul is bared
Speaks to me in times of fear
when darkness falls and death is near
Flows through every waking breath
and as I sleep it lies beneath
Catches every single tear
The greatest love is always here

There is something in each of us that listens to our deepest intentions and wishes. Not the superficial, but the element that calls us forth into the world and helps bring to life the most loving version of ourselves.

It can be a caring guide in dark times, and a loyal supporter to help us realise our dreams. It can show itself as compassion, kindness, encouragement, joy, creativity, determination, upliftment or courage.

It is always here through our waking and sleeping, our dreaming and not dreaming.

At some point we are going to run into our fear of death. Complete nothingness. The void.

Eventually we just meet it.

## NO MORE WAITING

The days you think you're waiting for are already here
if you create them for yourself and live without the fear

No more fear. Fear of anything.

Fear is the opposite of love. It strangles love's creativity. It holds us back from acts of kindness. It stops us speaking our truth and building a kinder and more inclusive world.

I spent years in debilitating frozen fear and a range of behaviours that amounted to hiding – from myself and others. Frozen in my body and stuck in rigid mental patterns that were about not being seen, feeling undeserving and having great doubt. It was so obvious and yet so deeply held at the same time that it kept me stuck in a way of being that was exhausting.

Facing our fears allows us to live more fully and step into our power. This is not the kind of power that we generally see in our collective. It is the power we hold as a loving and kind being who is in full possession of our gifts and using them wisely.

It means becoming increasingly strong in the presence of our inner demons. While this seems hard to do at first, we can come to see that our fear is the direction of our growth. Our fears guide us to what we need to overcome to realise our potential. Meeting our fears allows us to create more of what we want in our hearts, and not in our minds. What we create in ourselves we create in the world.

Living without fear is learning to be courageous. It's not always easy but we are much more fearless than our minds tend to think. Our hearts are so strong.

We go through our fears. From the small ones that ask us to keep learning and growing, to the big existential ones. At some point we meet our ultimate fear that we run from in a thousand different ways.

Minds love fear. Fear lives in the mind. Love lives in the heart. Eventually there is no fear.

~
SILENCE

## LISTEN

The silence in everything is singing to you
A love song

There is silence within song. In the most beautiful songs, in nature, in the fullest expression of our own individuality, in everything.

Even in our suffering it is somehow calling us home, even when that seems like a cruel joke. It is also the call to peaceful and loving action in the world, towards living in harmony with ourselves and others.

It speaks to us if we can listen, and it calls us on more and more, deeper and deeper. Back to what we are now and have always been.

It's a love song.

## THE BIRDS

The birds are singing out your name
They call you on to hear again
the deepest truth in which you know
all things must pass but only so
at the end of search and toil for wealth
one day you may just find yourself
in stillness with all thoughts surpassed
beyond all measure, free at last

Nature *is* our nature.

Flowers flower, trees grow and bloom. The birds sing as they have always done. They are you and you are them if you can listen to their song with all of your being.

We might touch this in moments of deep communion with nature. The majesty of high mountains; the aliveness of a coral reef or rainforest; the peace of a silent desert; the wonder of the night sky. All can touch our essential nature as an undivided part of nature itself.

When our mind settles down to something approaching stillness, it is possible for things to open. We tend to spend a lot of time working and searching outside of ourselves. We can do the same within our experience too. So much 'doing' and not so much 'being' can exhaust us on many levels.

There is another way to be amongst the human busyness. Free as a bird, nothing to be except ourselves exactly as we are: singing our song, feeling our joy, feeling our pain, rising again, everything arising and passing as it needs to. No resistance to anything. Everything possible and everything here as it is. Ourselves and our song.

Stillness amongst it all. The deep peace of our own being. True freedom is beyond all measure.

# A LITTLE SONG OF SILENCE

A little song of silence appeared in me one day
I listened very carefully, it had not a word to say
It grew and grew through many days 'til it was all around
I listened even closer, it didn't make a sound
I listened for the sound to come until the day had gone
When the sun came up again there was silence in the dawn
I listened for it in others when my own ears couldn't hear
When other folks thought 'What's the point?' I always heard it here
It crowded out belongings and feelings of desire
When it burnt up my emotions there was silence in the fire
One day it overwhelmed me like a sublime lover's kiss
Silence gone into itself – divine eternal bliss

Silence arrives in different ways to break the constant noise of our busy mind and lessen our attachment to experience. It can help us to discover more of who we are. While it doesn't come to everyone, we can do more to encourage it in ourselves and others, and to promote silence and contemplation as values. Silence can be both beautiful and powerful.

The notion of a really quiet mind was beyond my experience for a long time. Fortunately, the quiet that is underneath started to open up. I found that once my mind started to quieten down other things began to arise. They weren't all pleasant. Emotions, patterns, ideas, belief systems, desires and wants all came up for examination. It was all part of the journey back to who I am.

I'd be lying if I said I spent a lot of time in a place where there was genuine silence. Some days were wild and stormy but increasingly there was a distance between the noise and the silence from which it arose. Trying to get back to the sense of peace and silence in each moment is a practice and can be elusive.

Sometimes it is as simple as just falling into the silence that is already here, watching the sunset, or enjoying the early morning when the world is quiet. Eventually we come to recognise that silence more and more.

Our world is so dominated by the demands of our own minds and the collective mind. Although it is available to everyone, stopping to see what lies within us, or a search for deeper meaning is not a choice we all make. Some of us have no inclination whatsoever to inquire beyond our daily thoughts and habits. Fully identified with the mind, the possibility of silence and greater depth of being or how that can positively change our human experience, many of us live lives disconnected from who we truly are.

Why some of us find ourselves in a position to look deeper while others don't is a mystery. Some, with all the material resources they could ever need, strive for more and more and may never turn inwards. Some, who have little from a material perspective, live lives of simple contentment and abundance. Why so many are born into poverty without the chance to even think about the fullness of human existence is a reflection of how far we have still to travel.

It's not that our desires are bad, they just become beautiful in and of themselves, and we are ruled less by striving towards and running away from them. We see them more fully and more accurately. Of course, some pleasures are beautiful and are a gift of human existence. Some are outright harmful. How we relate to them becomes more important.

As we become defined less and less by our desires, or enter into better relationships with them, different needs come in. Healthier behaviours, and new desires for wellbeing, altruism, and fulfilment for ourselves and others are all part of our growth and maturity.

I found my attachment to belongings and the material world fell away. Material things I had previously felt a great affinity to were now perceived very differently. Still to be enjoyed, but ultimately seen for what they are – impermanent and not a source of genuine happiness. I spent a long time not wanting to really be in the material world and feeling a deep sense of disconnection from materialism and consumerism. Eventually there was a settling: to being in the world, but not of the world as a felt sense in my body rather than a concept in my mind. I found myself not turning away from the material world but deepening the respect I had always held for it. Deep gratitude for my personal circumstances and great appreciation for the source from where everything has come. The food we eat, the clothes we wear, water – everything.

The further we enter into the stillness, the more comes up for inquiry. Emotional content, repressed feelings and the reasons for our behaviours and tendencies. These can be deeply buried and can be personal and transpersonal. At the same time, we can also find joy, wonder and space to create the new.

Underneath it all is the silent space in which all things arise.

Ultimately silence is an aspect of who we are.

Deep silence is both a doorway to, and a quality of the truth.

## A PLACE IN MY HEART

There's a place in my heart the same as yours
where everything that went before
falls away and is no more
Where everything that's yet to come
is not to do and won't be done
Is peace and love that we all share
and calls you on if you would dare
to rest your mind 'til all is still
and come to peace as is love's will

We spend a lot of our time thinking about the past or the future. It can be a source of regret and anxiety. As a world-class ruminator, I learned to do both quite prodigiously. Fortunately, I also learned to start to take care of my mind and body more with greater kindness. It takes time and practice and it is a constant work in progress – as we all are. There are many beautiful practices and helpful people to support us if we care to look.

If we are able to settle into our being we will see our journey is not about the idea of who we have been in the past, or who we will be in the future, but about touching our deepest presence and a shared common human experience. We share the same fundamental nature as each other if we can only stop and learn to recognise it.

We cannot find the truth of who we are in our mind. We might find an idea of it there, as minds are good at ideas and concepts, but what we *really* are exists beyond our mind.

To rest in a quiet place where there are no thoughts of past or future is profoundly peaceful.

We all share the same essential nature. It is peace and love.

## SILENT FRIEND

Silence has become my friend
when everyone has gone
Reached a point I'd rather find
deep quiet and be alone

We need refuge. Refuge from our lives, refuge from the madness of the world, refuge from ourselves and the unhelpful dialogues we carry around.

There is a time to be out in the world and there is a time to be silent and alone in our experience. Time spent deeply in our inner world helps us to know who we are more fully.

Finding refuge in the company of caring and like-minded others is important. At times when I have felt like a stranger in my own life, I have been lucky to know I am not alone, and that even though they might not be in the same physical space as me, there are people all over the world who are dedicated to nurturing and helping our world. People who value their own inner journey and supporting others in theirs.

In the age of technology, we are increasingly together in our loneliness. In a different time we might be capable of being alone, but more fully together. Together, in that our sense of self is stronger, and together as part of the greater community of humanity. This is true togetherness.

We aren't ever truly alone even when we are by ourselves. We receive the unseen and mostly under-appreciated support of nature, as well as inner and outer friends.

There is an ultimate refuge in the truth of who we are.

## SHELTER FROM THE STORM

There is a quiet place inside
to where I go when all is wild
It's where I stand within the storm
that rages hard with thoughts that harm
where all the books that I have known
now make more sense than we are shown
We read too simply and make mistakes
and set ourselves as opposites
of two sides of a single stream
where love is still inside the dream

As easy as it might be to say everything is peace and light, the truth of the human experience is that we have a body and a mind, and it is with these that we live our lives and experience the world.

Waking up, growing up and self-inquiry are not all peaceful and light. As we look inwards and tap into the truth of what our body and mind do, including how we store our experience in both, all sorts of things can be released. It can get wild.

There is light in the darkness, peace in the conflict. The process of opening up to deeper experiences asks us to face long-held feelings, emotions and even experiences and material that are beyond our conscious awareness. This can include both the individual subconscious and the collective unconscious. The capacity to meet the depths of our experience with compassion and learn the lesson contained within it is essential. Otherwise we are likely to repeat our behaviours and our responses.

Literal interpretations of some traditions can ask us to surrender our lives to a higher power without owning our experience. Giving our sovereignty to an external authority denies us our own true power and responsibility. At the same time, it can overinflate our ego's ideas of who we are and set up all sorts of dialogues about ourselves and others. These then play out in our own inner lives and are scaled up grotesquely in the collective. Greater oppositional forces and separation is fuelling growing inequity, division, socio-political discord and environmental destruction. 'Othering' has become a dominant narrative which threatens our inner peace and efforts towards peace in the world.

There is a difference between our mind's idea of power and our true sense of self – which resides in our heart. Our heart-self doesn't work with opposition. Our minds love it.

Accepting the idea that we are opposites is to avoid the reality of our experience. Arriving at a place of inclusiveness where we are able to understand an ever-increasing degree of acceptance, despite holding different opinions and positions, is important. It is also fertile ground for resolving our differences and helping others come to a more integrated view.

Our experience is the dream inside the dreamer. It is possible to find stillness in the wildest storms. The totality in our unique expression. The eternal in the temporal.

~

DARKNESS

## I SURRENDER

I surrender, I'm exhausted, I've nothing left to give
I gave it all to someone else and now I have to live
A deeper truth for all to see is hiding in plain sight
and in the depths of darkness the still can see the light

Once we come to realise or experience we are not our mind, we can find ourselves in a place where we see how caught up we have been in an aspect of ourselves which is neither true or helpful. We can enter into the darkness of existential crisis through different times of life, or experiences that radically shift our perspective of who we are.

I've been exhausted through grief, despair and cathartic releases to the point that I have barely been able to get up for the day. I've also put a lot of time and effort, heart and soul into other people's ideas of who I am. We adopt so many roles in life and while they might change, being too defined by them can be unhelpful.

I also gave a lot of myself to my own idea of 'me' that wasn't always completely true. In some ways yes, and wonderfully so, but there was a deeper element of myself that I knew I didn't always acknowledge. A part of me that was more fully me, my heart wisdom, my personal truths and a deeper and more authentically powerful version of myself.

Authenticity in each of the roles we take on means being who we truly are. Hopefully at our best, but recognising that we can only ever make an effort in that direction and that from a higher perspective, we are exactly as we need to be right now in this moment.

Always being, always becoming. We are all works in progress.

Existentially we may experience a dark night of the soul. A time when it feels like life is totally pointless and meaningless. That no practice will work, our lives a barren wasteland, a desert of existence that is utterly devoid of meaning. All our energy and effort gets consumed into the death throes of the ego-mind and it exhausts us: physically, mentally, emotionally, psychically and spiritually.

Even during great suffering at any level of our being, there is relief in the unseen which holds it all. We can touch it in stillness, and recognising it when we are in the depths of despair can help us to move through it.

As dark as our experience may be there is ultimately light within it.

## UNRAVELLING

I feel like I'm unravelling
not sure which way to go
No direction travelling
can't say yes or no

Numbed out by the pain of the past
not sure which way to turn for the best
Can't yet see the next few hours
let alone the coming years

I cannot act for all the fear
my tears flow constantly
All the pain of all the world
is all inside of me

I know the things I've been before
and I just want them back
It surely never was this hard
to feel the love I lack

This is getting crazy now
I've lost a year and don't know how
Somewhere I would rather be
I cannot reach for the life of me

It would be the easiest thing
to slowly slip away
To melt again into the spring
as night slips into day

This is holy darkness
Nowhere left to turn
All my deeds and thoughts surpassed
Everything has gone

One day darkness next the light
I stand alone to fight the fight
Let me back into myself
or disappear to somewhere else

The sense of falling and falling deeper and deeper into the darkness and becoming consumed by it can be exhausting. The greater sense of self that you know yourself to be feels completely unattainable as your mind constantly tries to assert itself. The part of you that you always thought was in control is now seen as an impostor and it resists with everything it has got.

Trying to perform daily functions let alone make bigger decisions and see a clear way forward was difficult for a while.

I lost a lot of time in existential crisis, in being caught between trust and complete annihilation, and a sense that there was absolutely nothing I could do about it. I knew I had taken a big leap of faith and was living with the consequences of my decisions, as well as the changes taking place on every level of my being – none of which felt like they were working.

At the same time, trying desperately to get back to my true self underneath it all felt utterly futile, and the idea of disappearing off to somewhere else, an impossibility. There is truly nowhere to go.

Eventually though, we come to realise that we are never truly by ourselves and that we are being held up by existence itself – even when we think we are alone. There is always support if we only ask. Deep within us, from good friends, and from life itself. We support each other.

Faith is staying in your heart in the darkness.

## DESPAIR

Despair as I have never known
has settled in my heart
Affairs of mind and man have blown
and torn my world apart

It is easy to spend a lot of time in despair at the state of the world. The injustice; the inequity; the scale of suffering. The impact our lack of respect and understanding has had on the world can be hard to bear.

Internally there is the same despair as the mind desperately tries to resist the fact that it is not running the show. There is an element of desolation, a fall from grace and feelings that the wonder of life has gone. The personal world that has been torn apart cannot be put back together and both our inner and outer worlds are beyond hope.

All of this is the product of a mind that exists in separation from what *is*. It is the same mind that tears our external world apart day-to-day. The same collective unconscious that is the expression of millions of minds and does so much harm to our fellow humans, animals and to the planet.

Learning to care for our mind and its dark potentials is important.

Expressions of our heart rebuild our inner and outer worlds.

## LOVE OF THE HEART

There is no pain like love of the heart
It breaks and tears your world apart
When there's nothing more to take
it comes again once more to break
your shattered soul which has no more
lies broken ruined on the floor
and when you feel you can't go on
is loving warm like morning sun
Its warm embrace a caring friend
No beginning and no end

Following our heart, even when it hurts and breaks everything we have ever really known into pieces, is courageous. The pain can run so deep that we feel we have nothing left to sustain us. Nothing at all.

Ultimately, we can look into the depth of who we are as a soul and see that all the decisions we make are supported by something far greater. We are being called on by love, whether that is for our growth or our temperance.

The whole of creation is holding us up moment to moment. From the natural world, to the realms we don't believe in or that we dismiss with our mind, we exist in relationship to them all. There is always nurture and help on hand when we attune to it.

We continue to learn even through our most challenging experiences and, on some level, even through death itself.

Love is both the undoing of the old and the making of the new.

## ALONENESS

How did you know where to find me?
You asked with heart and gave so kindly
Told me in love and gentle of heart
Hold me above and shine like the stars
Took a long time, many roads did I wander
Through wild winter storms, rain, lightning and thunder
Sometimes a glimpse of sun through the rain
Your arms wrapped around me I sat with my pain
In time I've come to see more clearly
In darkness and heartbreak you held me so dearly
For aloneness is the price you pay
for love and truth to light your way

Being alone and being with ourselves deeply is a gift.

It is also a necessary part of the path of growth and inquiry. Without being able to be completely alone with ourselves, we aren't able to understand who we truly are and what we truly need in body, spirit and mind. To understand fully the relationship we have with ourselves makes us whole and more able to be in relationship with others more authentically.

There is also the aloneness of 'being'. An existential state of feeling completely disconnected from everything. It can feel as if we are just barely able to put one foot in front of the other, utter abandonment. Fortunately, we come to see that what we thought was aloneness was actually a process of emergence. We are supported through it by our deepest intentions and by love itself.

As we go through the transition we come to realise that we are alone, and yet at the same time, standing in the oneness of it all.

## A SMILE

A smile to know it's all okay
A smile inside to show the way
A smile to see after all the tears
To know you're loved through all your fears
A smile that never goes away
A smile of love that's here to stay

The truth is we are already home. Our inner smile tells us so even when our experience is claiming otherwise. It is the smile of deep compassion within us that can hold it all.

I've touched some dark moments as we all do. Pain is pain. Suffering is suffering. To have someone else be able to witness it all and hold it with love is a powerful human experience, one which can be deeply healing and transformative. The smile of another human being showing compassion and love for you, all of you, is beautiful. Counsellors, therapists, healers and teachers who can do this are human wonders. To see a smile at the end of the storm to welcome you home, or a smile of deep recognition of the truth in each other is a treasure.

The smile of caring friends, including those inside us, is sometimes all the encouragement we need to keep going.

Learning to receive our own smile taking care of us is self-compassion.

A smile of unconditional love.

Our smile back to the world.

Awake.

~
RISING

## THE DOOR OF MY HEART

This is the door of my heart
It is open to all
Firstly it is open to me, all of me
The broken and unbreakable
The lost and found
The hungry and thirsty
The willing and able
The lazy and dirty
The pieces of me I shut away
too scared to see the light of day
The others that adore the light
who keep on dancing through the night
The door of my heart is open wide
and welcomes one and all inside


*Thank you, Ajahn Brahm*

Increasing our ability to extend our heart to all aspects of ourselves is helpful.

We tend not to turn towards and learn to care for the different faces of our pain but instead run from them. Shame, anger, grief, self-loathing, collapse, catastrophising. Underneath these are their opposites – authenticity, power, joy, compassion, solidity and equanimity. Eventually we don't need to go through the dark places as we learn to find and nurture our positive qualities in the moment.

We can also find our purpose and our gifts and give ourselves to them more fully. Finding and shining our light is illuminating.

We're often not as kind and supportive of ourselves as we could be. To be kind to ourselves and all of who we are helps us do the same for others.

Compassion for all our pieces, the broken and the unbreakable, makes us whole.

## RISE ABOVE

Come and take a look at me
What you thought I'd never be
The parts of me that got shut down
were ridiculed as dreaming clowns
Were closed away and kept below
so far down I'd never know
But deep inside they cannot stay
They long to see the light of day
For now they come to rise above
And as they rise they rise with love

Some external voices become internal voices. My inner voices helped to beat me up, they controlled me and stopped me from being who I am. They frequently sabotaged my dreams.

There was one that tended to be quite loud. For me it was the one that said you cannot be who you are: powerful, in possession of all your gifts in a loving and kind sense and making a positive difference. That having dreams of something greater than this current reality for myself and for humanity was wrong.

Rumination became my defence and I internalised and chewed over what I knew, rather than having the courage to communicate my thoughts, views and needs. In terms of expression and action in the world, it had to be perfect or not at all. It's an unhelpful way of being. A lot of energy is internalised and it accumulates in the body.

Keeping it all in became a bit of a problem. Pushing things down is depression. As with anything suppressed, the deeper it is pushed down the more it is likely to explode when it comes out. Rageful tears, grief for things unsaid and held back when I knew better were all inside.

Authenticity is always available. We can easily lose sight of it as we develop, as our need for safety and attachment overrides our need for authentic connection to who we are. Fortunately our true self is there waiting for us if we can learn to let go of some of the unhelpful patterns we adopted to make sure we were looked after in our early developmental stages of life. It is a process of growing into and embodying who we always were and what we were meant to do. It is re-learning to connect to ourselves.

At the collective level we need more dreamers, the ones who can envision greater possibilities for the world and inspire change in the hearts of others. If we can match it with great action, kind words and loving presence we can change the world for good.

Those with a narrow and pessimistic view of who we are as humans are only telling their own story. They miss the deeper truth: that we all have the capacity for greatness of insight and compassion, and can play our part in waking up, cleaning up our planet and raising our individual and collective consciousness.

## WHAT WE THOUGHT

What we thought we ought to be isn't us at all
They're ideas that we were told
that keep us playing small
What we are is so much more
than all the dreams we kept in store
Long held inside and shut away
but held beneath they cannot stay
They will lift you up again
to take you to a higher plane
Way, way, way up high
Where love is endless as the sky

I thought I ought to be something I was not. It worked well, really well, for a long time but ultimately it didn't. It was a much smaller version of who I am and while it served me at many levels, on others it kept me from speaking and stepping into my truth.

Our society is well-structured to keep people in work they'd rather not do, and often working for organisations or corporations that are not serving our individual or collective health and wellbeing. For the most part, it is not helping us to find and grow our most authentic sense of self. Our individual and collective dreams and potentials are vastly greater than our reality.

What could we become and achieve as humans and as humanity with greater love and greater vision?

## YOUR TRUSTED GUIDE

Return and see these words as truth
Your journey home, your doubtless proof
Your compass and your trusted guide
'Love is to live and not to hide'

What if we stopped hiding who we really are? Life lived deeply is raw, sometimes exciting, sometimes painful, but it is full and beautiful for it, and we learn compassion and gratitude as we go.

I lived a large part of my life lost or in hiding. Compliant yet detached from my deeper abilities and passions, I presented a view to the world of competence and goodness – but not truth and authenticity. While that life was being lived, a greater process was underway. Reading and learning experiences were leading me further and further down a path of self-inquiry, of growing up, embodiment, self-realisation and deeper learning.

I certainly didn't share or open up to the fullness of my experience or understanding. Often because I was derided for the views I held and the choices I made, and I had a great fear of the judgement of others. There was a growing difference between the face I showed to the world and what I knew deep within. Not what I thought, but what I knew in my heart.

I was very fortunate to have had a good education – amazing opportunities for learning, travel and work – but the education system and familial and societal expectations were the dominant forces in my choices about work and the kind of life I was meant to lead. This is an all too familiar story in our collective and it is possible to spend a lifetime following it or being defined by it.

Showing our deepest self, our heart, to others takes courage and vulnerability. It is our greatest pain and our greatest joy. Being seen for who we truly are as a soul is an intimate act. It is being seen for all of who we are, the layers we use as protection, our light and our darkness, but especially our essence.

We tend to neither show ourselves nor allow ourselves to see, or be seen by, another deeply. We aren't taught to do so, and it can be difficult to find this sense of intimacy in the ways we grow up learning, and amongst the ideas of a society that is built on superficiality and often unhelpful conventions.

If our lives lived in fullness of heart were an example of what we could do for others, what differences could we make to those we are able to influence?

Living as love in the world is a process of coming home.

Our heart is our guide.

## LOVE TO FLY

All the things I longed to find
were in my heart for all this time
Locked away behind the fear
the hurt and pain I've held so dear
A butterfly that spreads its wings
a bird that finds its voice to sing
don't think so much about their fate
the death that one day lies in wait
Free to dance and float on high
for in their hearts they love to fly

We are much more free than we tend to think.

I thought about death for a long time. Too long really. An inner dialogue that said: 'You're going to die and you won't have done what you longed to do in your heart. You've failed. Useless.'

The 'I' that thinks about death isn't who you really are. It's the part of you that is scared of coming to an end. It's the voice of the ego. It's the ultimate distraction but it has a thousand faces and games to play.

At some point you might just be who you are without the fear of death, and without the voices that tell you all the ways you can't be who and what you really are.

Our gifts are already here. It's just that we identify so much with our fears and reasons why we can't show ourselves that we lock them up. We can learn to see we are not our fears, our pain or any other elements of our suffering – whether our own, our parents' or that of humanity.

We can open the gifts that are expressions of our soul. Insights that allow us to give more of our true selves to the world. We can find treasures beyond value. The great colours of our being and the beauty of our song.

The deeper the insight the greater our wingspan.

We are already free to fly.

## ALL THE THINGS

All the things I thought were me
have all been left behind
The small, old, outgrown thoughts I had
were just my crazy mind
What's to see after the bliss
when everything lights up?
And you're still here in emptiness
while love has filled your cup

And you're not even moving
though the actions are still there
The actor just a movement
on a stage that's always bare
What's the play and who's the player?
Or are they just the same?
And does it really matter
if Love is both their name?

Once we start to see what we really are, we come to realise that a lot of our old way of being was just a series of patterns stuck on repeat.

To feel our cup filled with a sense of love, beauty and empowerment becomes the source from which we can give to others.

Divinity is both imminent and transcendent. It is who we are, how we live our lives, and the witness to it all.

The more we rest on the stage, the greater the play and the players in it.

Existence is the masterpiece.

## STORIES

Wind blows through this cluttered house
clearing all the stories out
Windows open, the storm is wild
Walls will stand just for a while
Even they will soon be gone
The roof falls down, you come undone
Finally the floor gives way
Wide open to the light of day

How many stories do we have about ourselves? All the conditioned responses, familiar ways of being, fears, default patterns and thought loops. Our inner world can get pretty crowded with stories and definitions. I have lived in a few large and powerful stories about myself. They haven't always been a good home environment.

When we start to see them for what they are, they start to lose their power and hold over us. This is especially true of the ones that are unsupportive and sometimes destructive. Replacing them with helpful narratives and strong foundations is a much better way to build a house. The structures that keep us imprisoned can be dismantled. Our true strength and light are inside us all along. Dropping the stories helps us live more freely.

Eventually there are no stories.

## FORGIVENESS

Forgiveness for the deeds I've done
and more for those I haven't
Words not meant to hurt someone
Thoughts I wished I hadn't
For all the times I looked away
afraid to see the truth
The one that I could never face
forgiveness for myself

True forgiveness is for ourselves.

It is learning to be kind again to all of who we are in spite of the things we have done or left undone. Guilt, shame, anger and other often unwanted emotions are the products of past experiences. Frequently though, it is the repeating and additional dialogues that keep us attached to the experience, and which don't permit us to feel it fully and proportionately – to learn and move through it. Looking deeply allows us to see from a higher and more compassionate perspective. It also helps us to not live in the past and recreate the same unhelpful dialogues in the future.

My inner critic is quietly hostile, often not so quietly. It is a pernicious self-dialogue that has held me back, is hypercritical in spite of some degree of objective achievement, and at its worst has been a terrible hindrance on my creativity and any real sense of authentic, wise action. I've also held on to bitterness and anger for events and deeds that were not of my making, nor were they mine to own. We do the same in our collective consciousness on a grand scale.

Ultimately I just didn't want to feel so relentlessly worn down by such an unforgiving inner voice. True forgiveness, as opposed to the idea of it, has a felt sense in the body and there is a more genuine feeling of ease. The critical dialogue calms down too.

The internalised voice of the judgement of others and our own quickness to judge ourselves can be quietened. Profound self-love is on the other side. Self-confidence that is born of the heart rather than the mind, and a willingness to stand out for the right reasons, is there with it.

Self-forgiveness at the deepest levels is a recognition that we have caused harm to others throughout our lives. Also, that as humans we cannot live in a way that doesn't cause some degree of harm, however high our intentions. The insight gives us ever greater intentions towards kindness, a deeper understanding of the interconnected nature of things, and allows greater compassion and peaceful action to flow.

Collective forgiveness is the ability to recognise the harm we have inflicted on each other and the Earth, and to take steps towards wholeness and integration. Forgiving others and starting anew creates space for peace, tolerance and reconciliation.

We can always seek forgiveness from others when we know in our heart it is right to apologise. Speaking honestly from the heart is helpful.

We can forgive ourselves. For everything. It is one of the kindest things we can do.

What we forgive in ourselves we forgive in others.

It is a powerful way to come to peace. In ourselves, our families, communities and between nations.

## LET GO

Let go and cry your divine tears
Let them come, all of them
Every one for right and wrong
the heartbreak, fear, the perfect song
the grief, the loss, the mind in confusion
the hopes, the dreams, the shattered illusion
the natural world, man-made injustice
the joys of life and the ones we miss
Compassion for yourself alone
Kindness now for everyone
For when your tears are fully cried
there is no place for love to hide

We push them down and don't feel our feelings. This is especially true in cultures where we are told that crying is a weakness. Contrary to popular belief it is normal and healthy. Holding emotions in takes a lot of energy.

Tears can be beautiful tears too. Why not be moved by beautiful people and experiences, words and actions? There are also the joys of life; birth; great acts of kindness; the natural world in all its wonder to behold. These are everyday miracles that we overlook too easily.

Once you've cried the tears for yourself there is a deeper sense to which it is possible to open: the collective that resides in each of us. The scale of human and animal suffering in the world is great and can be overwhelming to admit.

When we open to the depth of our own suffering and recognise the same exists in others, that it is part of both the human condition and of all living beings, we come to compassion. All of the world's suffering is in us and so is the end of it. Compassion for ourselves grows as we recognise our own suffering and it becomes a source to share with others.

Kindness and loving action can grow from sorrow. Ultimately we can realise love doesn't have to come from suffering, nor does it need to hide.

Love is here to be given freely in this moment.

Let go. Don't hide.

## LIFE WELL-LIVED

This grief has been an anguished friend
On which I've become reliant to depend
It reminds me of just how much I lost
And what I thought had mattered most
But now I have to say goodbye
To treasured tears and glistening eyes
To give of all I have to give
An open-hearted life well-lived

If we live our lives attached to a few strong emotions and patterns we limit our experience and opportunity. They keep us stuck and confined.

For most of my life I have had three defaults: anxiety, grief and melancholy. They have always been there. Sometimes just walking alongside me, their voices a steady stream in my ear. When big decisions needed to be made these three friends got very loud. Sometimes too loud. It turns out these old friends have very old roots deep within me – familial, collective and learned.

Once I started to become more and more aware of the impact they were having on my behaviour and my being, I started looking more deeply into them. With some wonderful help and wise words, I realised underneath the anxiety is authenticity, under the grief is love and under the melancholy is joy.

They are all aspects of an illusion of separation from love that we create in ourselves. We cannot be separate from what we are, as much as our minds tell us otherwise.

Our old friends can be difficult to see at first as they are such a familiar part of our internal landscape, but once we say goodbye and give thanks for their support, new beautiful friends come. The new ones are quiet, but they are true. They can be encouraged to grow louder too.

Then came the grief for the old dying. My old sense of self which clung on. The grief for that part of me and all the things it did became a bottomless pit which I fell into. Eventually that grief just became an add-on to the default sense of melancholy and anxiety that stopped me from moving forward. I was as much attached to the grief as I was to the old sense of self for which it pined.

Saying goodbye to my friend 'the grief' was hard. The memories that he keeps alive are beautiful and treasured. He is always there and I love him and all he holds, but he can't stand in the way of what is emerging. A life well-lived can't be held back by addiction to one deep-rooted emotion.

## THE CHANGE WE NEED

The change we need's not all outside
It's in our minds where the demons hide
For every demon we set free
leads our heart to liberty

We all have personal demons and share collective demons. Elements in us that are unhelpful and lead us away from the truth of who we are.

At some point in a human life we are going to run into our shadow. Maybe we run into the collective shadow? The dark potentials that exist in us manifest in the collective. The same is true of our greatest potentials.

Waking up asks us to looks at our demons. To recognise them and the power they exercise over us. To set them free and not be defined by them. To know that they exist in all of us, but not to strengthen them.

We can steadily reshape our inner and outer world to stop feeding our inner and collective demons. We can reduce so much unnecessary suffering through becoming more aware of our attention and where we place it, to help train our minds, to nurture our positive qualities and relate better to our less helpful ones.

With less energy given to escaping or fighting demons, we can give more of ourselves to our greatest potentials.

The heart has no demons.

## MORE TO THE EYE

There's more to this than meets the eye
No more a case of do or die
Could you just bring yourself to be
love in everything you see
All the seeds you hold within
The good, the bad, the ugly as sin
are all there to be held with love
for the simple purpose of
knowing those we focus on
will come to life and will be done

What we focus on becomes our reality.

Our future exists as potentials within us waiting to be brought into being. This is true from our own habitual thought patterns, to what we want to see and create in the world.

If we focus on the unhelpful parts of ourselves and compound the thoughts with our judgements, we are on the road to self-destruction and sabotage. We do it to ourselves and we do it in our families and communities.

We all have parts of us that we might not like so much, but we can accept them, recognise their origins, and learn to be with them constructively. Our human negativity bias tends to keep us in the wrongness of who we are by either trying to frantically escape our uncomfortable feelings and bad habits or indulging them. In both cases they have control over us rather than us coming to find a more useful relationship with them.

I got stuck trying to escape some uncomfortable thoughts and experiences, but in trying so hard became bound to them. We all have them but reclaiming our sovereignty, our choices and learning to feel our body helps us to become less defined by our difficulties and traumas. Compassionate self-inquiry helps us to accept who we are, why we are that way, and most importantly to reclaim our essence.

At the same time, focusing on our inner qualities that are sustaining and helpful builds those elements within us and makes us stronger. Cultivating helpful qualities also allows us to grow our internal support systems. We find strength to overcome adversity; equanimity in the face of difficult situations; self-support and compassion to create a solid and caring presence for ourselves and others.

Focused attention is also how we nurture our talents and bring our dreams into existence. Losing years to self-judgement, sabotage and fear is harder than turning towards it all and meeting it with compassion and the will to overcome and learn from it.

Focusing on the present moment helps us to overcome difficult experiences and live our lives more fully. We step out of our sufferance, our definitions and into our greatness.

Tending to our goodness and our abilities helps them to thrive.

## CAN'T HOLD BACK

I can't hold back there's so much love
for each soul below, each soul above
Nothing bound and nothing chained
No gift unfound, no love restrained

It can be difficult to uncover our true gifts and realise our greatest potentials – let alone to give them the opportunities to grow to their greatest extent and to offer them in loving service to others.

Economic and education systems that tend towards homogeneity and conformity stifle potential and creativity. Too much focus on material wealth and an attention economy that diverts us away from ourselves and our highest callings is stunting our individual and collective potential and is contributing to humanity's shadow.

What if we were all in possession of our greatest talents and could offer them altruistically? What is possible for the world if our focus shifts towards human wellbeing and reaching our highest potentials? How many great leaders, inspirational artists, writers, painters, poets, healers, policy geniuses, conscious business people and peacemakers are out there in the world and can be developed with the right insight and under the right conditions? What can the world look like for future generations?

Economies and education systems that cultivate gifts, wellbeing and greater inner qualities; the ability to care for and support our highest selves and our planet; to celebrate diversity as part of unity rather than homogeneity: these are all possible.

We can teach and learn how to love and flourish.

## THE GREAT WIDE OPEN

Somewhere out in the great wide open
Where hearts are kind and minds aren't closed
Somewhere beyond the far horizon
At last you're free and no one knows

The gap between our expressed ideals and the truth of what is happening in the world is enormous.

Over the last several thousand years our societies have set up various ideas of 'other' on which we can justify a myriad of behaviours, ideas, campaigns and policies, many of which deny our common humanity and in some cases our basic human rights. At its worst this results in death, division, displacement and suppression.

It is closed minds and hearts that feed on and perpetuate these ideas and beliefs. From international relations and geopolitics, to economies and our increasingly dysfunctional political systems and policies, we have lost sight of our shared humanity and interconnectedness.

If we could all tap into a more generous heart and open-minded way of being we could change the world. We urgently need to encourage this in all our leaders and especially our future leaders.

Beyond the ideas of the collective is the truth of who you really are. Here there are no closed minds or hearts.

Hiding in plain sight. No one except you knows you are free.

## FREE THE CHILDREN

The tears that I have sat and cried
were for the world that lives inside
Every tear for every child
the same as me who left the wild
The love of lost eternity
when all are one and all are free

We are a reflection of the world and how we see the world is a reflection of who we are.

The true innocence of childhood; freedom of expression; wild, joyful unknown adventure; exploration of potential and playfulness are the birthright of every human. Joy is an essential quality within us which can be rediscovered and allowed out to play. We can be free to feel young at heart at any age.

We grow up but our inner child stays with us, although we can lose sight of them in many ways. The world can be a serious and traumatic place and we can hide our children away and forget about the gifts they keep for us.

Society seems to be increasingly focused on making children into model citizens, compliant consumers and test-performers. Children are becoming more anxious in response to their circumstances, the increasing stress of their parents and the incessant demands of our society and culture. Most of us are on the treadmill of the desires of others, happily telling ourselves we need more and more, and that we are not enough.

What if we were all free to be who we really are? Underneath the layers we put on either as coping mechanisms or adopted behaviours? It is impossible not to take them on to some degree and it is part of learning and growing, indeed our survival depends on it. However, our survival strategies can maladapt. The coping mechanisms that protected us can become restrictions on our ability to grow throughout our lives and, at worst, can form the basis for addictions.

I left my inner child behind, life was serious and it stayed serious long after the events had passed. My inner child stayed neglected and shut away for a long time. I didn't even allow myself to properly care for that part of me.

We can also relate to our thoughts as children. They too need our care and kind attention.

We are not separate. We know and feel this when we are young, and we touch it when we are at our most innocent and vulnerable. It is a tender place. When we are at our most creative and playful we are closest to what we are. The solutions to many of our problems are probably best found through the eyes of a child. Forgiving of each other, caring and inclusive, children show us these beautiful qualities and they are wonderful examples to follow.

What conditions are we creating for our children? The children within, and the children of the world.

Caring for our children is essential. Teaching them love and kindness is for all of us.

Setting our children free is a gift.

## ORDINARY GODS

Ordinary gods we are
Falling on through time
Slow uncovering of our hearts
The work of life divine

Seen not once a million times
The truth of cosmic order
Breaking through the lines of mind
Until there are no borders

Part of growing is to slowly uncover our heart. To find its unique expression, its fullness, its joy, its courage, its strength and tenderness. To slowly take off all the layers we put over our hearts: the ones we put on to protect ourselves, those that keep us away from ourselves, and those that keep us away from others. It can be a lifetime's work, or we can just open.

Our minds put borders in places where none really exist.

A limitless heart is our greatest potential.

## TEARS FOR HUMANITY

There are times when I look deep inside
when all I see are tears I've cried
The more I look the more I find
that most of them were for my mind
which held so close to bygone days
of different times and outgrown ways
of things which we're so strictly told
but now seem broken, hard and cold
Now love is where it's always been
and when I sit and look within
the tears still come but not for me
the tears are for humanity
For everything that lies outside
is in my heart and cannot hide

Through the process there are tears, lots of tears, unshed tears for past hurts, for fears and experiences that we held onto in our body because we couldn't express feelings appropriately or safely. Tears of confusion for what is happening internally, tears of grief for the old sense of self that is falling away.

There is a point at which we get beyond ourselves and our own suffering. We still end up releasing and growing. We recognise our suffering, hopefully a little more skilfully and less self-indulgently, but the heart can still release quite spontaneously when touched deeply.

It can happen as part of loving-kindness or compassion meditations when we start to open up to the reality of our suffering and its depth. We might realise how much we hold on to it, often unnecessarily. We may come to see much of it as long-held, personal and ancestral.

Beyond that is the suffering of others and of the whole of humanity. Opening to that is hard. A crushing sense of the extent of suffering occurring in the world in this very moment can be too much to bear. Underneath it is great compassion for oneself and for all beings. We recognise that all the causes of that suffering also exist within us. It is also the wellspring from which action and determination to help end them arises. Knowing our suffering is the suffering of others is an important step towards caring for our common humanity.

This insight is the basis for making peace. There is no difference between the suffering of mothers and families on either side of conflicts who lose children and loved ones in acts of war and violence. It is also the foundation on which a new humanity can be built. Without looking within and coming to understanding, we will continue to create disharmony in ourselves and in the world. Fortunately the reverse is also true, and by looking deeply into ourselves we are able to positively change the worlds within and around us.

Humanity is in your heart.

~
SOUL

## FREE

I stand here free to give my gifts
The ones I thought that I had left
The ones that we all know are true
As they're for me, they are for you

This is what I came to teach
To live in truth while others preach
This is what I always was
Though I forgot, its name is love

Love is what we are as souls. Our unique manifestation of a greater consciousness with all its potential and qualities.

Though we may find ourselves far away from this innate capacity and insight, we are already integrated and full and are able to touch that aspect within us at any time. Our soul is always whole and not separate or cut off from who we are by our circumstances, thoughts or life situation. It is our sense of separation and our reactions to it that is the cause of much of our individual and collective suffering. To stand in our wholeness as souls and to know we are deeply connected, is both liberating and empowering.

We are always free to take the journey back to our heart, the path of our soul. It is a turning inward, a realisation of what we truly are and have always been. We come to know again that we are one with everything.

Our potential for transformation and its impact on those we influence is hard to overstate. We are a flicker of our full brightness. Individually and collectively we can come to a greater understanding of love. The intentions and behaviours that are forged from that insight and by cultivating those states have the power to transform our world. This is not superficial. It is integral to a shift in consciousness and towards the greater wellbeing of humanity and the Earth.

We are helped by reminders throughout our life of who we are at our best, what we are able to achieve and what we want to realise at the deepest levels of our intention and natural ability. We are kind, compassionate, powerful, intuitive and creative. Those qualities are who we truly are, though most of us tend to touch these states rather than inhabit them. Although we may lose sight of them through our conditioning and life experience they are always available. We can access them through presence, and aligning to our deepest intentions. So too, our ability to connect with our essence is already within us and inside our bodies. In doing so we come to embody our original wholeness as a free-flowing expression of love and kindness. Our own light.

The love that we are, we can give to ourselves and then to others.

It is a path of love and realisation for all.

Love is the light.

# DYING TO ONESELF

The grief of dying to oneself
I lost my heart in someone else
Found truth nobody can ignore
Still here I stand no other shore

Screams of pain from deep inside
An existential flood and tide
My heart ripped out while here I stand
And stopped in terror death's cold hand

My body not in my control
My mind was gone I saw my soul
Memories of a different time
Still alive their power shines

My broken mind's confused belief
My body folds, consumed by grief
Can't get up and fight again
What's to fight when love will win?

The time I spent inside death's door
Waiting for life to come once more
Not all lost it calls you on
Life and death now seen as one

The deepest wisdom of your soul
That never fails and won't grow old
Is always here though hard we grieve
Lives are lost – our souls don't leave

We are more than a body and a mind. A lot more. Our mind might try and convince us otherwise but we know it to be true. Our bodies have a natural intelligence that we tend to live disconnected from. So too, our mind's potential is far greater than we realise. Understanding the connection between body, spirit and mind can be the work of a lifetime.

It is possible to experience the depth of who we are through the body. Stored energies and cellular memories can be released through different modalities, treatments and induced states. We are able to increase our mental capacities and even see what we are both before and beneath our mind. We can liberate our soul through our body.

Periods of death and transformation during our lives are normal. They can be superficial, the ordinary transitions of life, or they can be profound changes to our psyche and sense of who and what we are. Whenever there is a death there is a transformation. A period of integration where we learn our lessons from the past and take them forward into the future. This can happen in all the phases of our life as we mature from one stage to another.

It is possible to feel as if we are reliving past experiences in the present moment as we uncover our deeper selves. It is a space of inquiry, growth and integration.

Ultimately we come to a lived understanding that we are part of an endless cycle of death and rebirth. That it happens in nature and that it happens to all things. We are a continuous process of being and becoming. This is life itself.

The insight of no death is a liberation. There is no more fear. As hard as the mind hangs on to the idea that there is some finality, that is just the mind's journey. It is not who we are.

For all the many beliefs and cultures that we can draw on, most of us intuitively sense that we have a deeper essence to our being that goes beyond the physical and the mental patterns through which we define ourselves. Many traditions recognise the existence of a soul and even its transmigration from one incarnation to another.

We tend to live within a narrow definition of who we are. What if we could encourage an understanding that allows us to be who we are more fully in this present life? In full possession of our greatest gifts and understandings? We grieve the past and worry about the future in ways that stop us from stepping into what we know deep inside us. We grieve for lives lost, those of others and even our own, instead of drawing on them for inspiration.

Our soul essence and wisdom transfers from lifetime to lifetime.

# WALKING HOME

One day all the tears will stop
It isn't yours and never was
The pain which you will leave behind
An echo of a different time

It doesn't all belong to you
You took it on for others who
didn't know the reasons why
And in terror fled to die

All were killed one by one
Love confronted by the gun
In front of you for you to see
You left hanging, a cedar tree

You caught them all as each they left
And walked them to their peaceful end
Took their souls and led them home
Loved them all as if your own

Of all the suffering we may feel, some of it is ours but much of it can belong to others. Even though we take it on, to recognise its true source and let it go can help us to better understand why we behave in certain ways, allowing us to open up to who we are without it. Our true self.

To be able to touch experiences with kindness, to find the insight underneath them and re-emerge, is a gift. We can do this physically, mentally, emotionally and spiritually. We can come to understand that we live in different times and worlds, and that they exist in and through us.

We can open to our deepest soul experiences, the beautiful and the difficult. Powerful elements of ourselves that we cut off or deny lie hidden in our being. Fragments of old experiences that can help us to understand who we are as souls can help us grow. The wisdom that can emerge from these insights contains important elements of what we need to learn. To really be in touch with love as a soul opens us to a richer experience of life here and now.

Collectively, we have been killing each other for thousands of years because we haven't understood the deeper nature of reality. This is the karmic wheel. Love helps to transform and bring completion.

There are some who are able to see, be with and transmute the pain of old experiences to facilitate a return to wholeness. Great, compassionate beings who perceive with their hearts help us to understand and change the collective consciousness one person at a time. They walk between worlds, see with their hearts and guide our souls on their journeys.

We have all been here before.

## ALIVE AND WELL

I woke that day a condemned man
I knew my fate as it began
My crime to write with words of truth
To give account of what I knew

Convicted by a judge of treason
For love held higher than pure reason
All the things for which I'd stood
For kindness, peace, the right and good

Held in chains a darkened cell
Tortured for what I couldn't tell
Final days the last goodbyes
My children's tearful pleading eyes

An execution's public show
I saw it coming the final blow
And in the terror the holy dove
The last word of my life was 'love'

They knew what they had done was wrong
They couldn't bear the wise and strong
I saw myself in all their eyes
A rush of light, regretful cries

The times for which the truth I died
The lives I lost for which I cried
For times I thought I'd burn in hell
I know my soul's alive and well

It never left it just moved on
And now once more again has come
To try to set the world on fire
With love and words to take us higher

## SHAMAN

My shaman's here to walk me home
He knows my soul, my flesh and bone
My loving heart my deep desire
My earth, air, water, space and fire

Open up and bring your drum
Journey with your ancient song
Your rattle, guides, ecstatic trance
Your flowers, stones and sacred plants

Dive into the other worlds
Return with insights to be told
Rise back up and shine your heart
The truth of which we all are part

Everything is here right now
All the things you need to know
Everything you've ever been
All the things one day will be

You don't forget, it's deep in you
The wisdom that's alive and true
We all have loving sacred power
To use in every waking hour

Return and claim your loving gift
You never died you never left
My shaman's here to walk me home
To love the truth and all as one

# THE PHOENIX

Once you've seen yourself in all
Your life is going to change
To wake up in the dream at last
And know it's all the same

Everything you knew before
Will all be cast aside
Burning pain exposed and raw
Waits for the soothing tide

Moving through the darkness
Your world is stripped away
Burnt reduced to ashes
An old life in decay

Then to wake your phoenix
Raise it from the ground
From ashes of illusion
The fire of love is found

It doesn't make it easy
And the fire of love still burns
We just keep on believing
To love our soul returns

The phoenix never truly dies
It changes on its way
Ash and fire one and the same
Dark night is love's new day

What we perceive day-to-day is like a dream. It really is.

Once we start to recognise the truth of who we are, the old version gets deconstructed. It happens at every level of our being. The body and mind are restructured. Old emotions are released, our psychology changes, belief systems are challenged and new understandings emerge. It is as if consciousness wakes up to itself and its true nature, and then clears out everything that is not aligned with that expression of consciousness. All of it happens in a space of deep love – even if it doesn't always feel that way.

It's an existential crisis that cannot be resolved on the level of the mind. Mine became very busy throwing out all sorts of stories: from madness to thoughts of imminent death, to floods of old emotions, ideas and beliefs. This is the fire of transformation. Love in its destructive aspect burns away what is no longer needed and at the same time is a catalyst for transformation to create the new.

The mythological phoenix deliberately throws itself into the fire in an act of destruction of the old to re-emerge as the new, rising from the ashes. This is the journey of the soul from separation to integration, from individuality to individuation. It is also the fire of passion for the new creation.

This goes in cycles that operate on a much deeper level than many of us tend to be aware of. Death and renewal are the cycle of life. What is death really, other than a change of form?

Even when it's totally dark, there is light in the darkness.

Raise your phoenix.

~
CREATIVITY

## BEFORE CREATION

What can you see on the clearest day?
What can you hear when there's nothing to say?
What can you feel when there's no sensation?
What can you know before creation?

Everything manifests from the unmanifest.

Entering into the stillness and the void with our highest intentions helps us to align with our greatest sense of who we are.

We already know our destiny if we quieten ourselves enough to listen. It is our most heartfelt desire. This can change over the course of a lifetime as we become more aware of the dreams we have for our lives. We bring our destiny into creation by seeing it clearly with our hearts and living from our deepest intentions.

Creativity comes from a unique space within us. We are all naturally creative and have our own individual means of expression to pursue, encourage, celebrate and bring to fruition.

Truly creative endeavours come from allowing space for new patterns and ideas to emerge. If we are stuck in repeating patterns there is less room for new ideas to be expressed. From small ideas to large-scale leaps, our ability to create new expressions is part of the transformation of our collective consciousness. From music and the arts, to scientific breakthroughs and great social changes, creative geniuses have recognised a sense of inspiration that is beyond the rational mind.

Creative genius is a divine gift.

Our daily lives can become beautiful expressions of our own creativity. We write the song of our lives a day at a time. If our own songs can lead us towards greater love and harmony, then they can also lift up others and help us all to play our unique part in the play of consciousness itself. Our songs help to connect us all. They build understanding and can open the door of insight for others – if they are willing to walk through.

There is a place before creativity. It points us to the ultimate truth, and at the same time, is gone.

~
TRUE NATURE

## I KNOW

I know earth is in me and I am earth
I know water is in me and I am water
I know fire is in me and I am fire
I know air is in me and I am air
I know space is in me and I am space
I know peace is in me and I am peace
I know love is in me and I am love
I know my suffering is the suffering of all beings
The 'I' that knows isn't even me
The 'I' that knows no eyes can see

The earth in our food is the earth that we walk on, it is the earth in every cell of our bodies, and the Earth to which all our physical forms will return. It is the solidity of our bones, our minerals, our soils, trees and plants.

The water in our body is the same as the water in our rivers and aquifers. The water in our tea is the water in the clouds, the water in our emotions. It is our mighty glaciers, rivers, seas and oceans, and also the qualities of movement and fluidity.

The fire in the hearth is the fire in our bellies, the fire in our hearts, the fire in our forests and the fire of power and change in ourselves. It is the fire of determined effort and transformation.

The air is the sky, our atmosphere, our breath, our life force, our words. Air as our breath and spirit is an indicator of our state of being and a powerful source of insight and healing.

The space inside of us makes up most of what we are. We are the great spaces: from our wide-open landscapes and the space within atoms, to the numinous and the vast expanse of the cosmos.

Only by stopping and looking deeply can we see that we are our environment: the earth, the water, the fire, the air and infinite space.

We share more with our fellow beings than we recognise. From DNA and the range of emotions we all feel, to the same basic needs. We are not so different.

We know it directly when we get past thoughts of 'I'.

We experience it when there are no thoughts.

## PLANTING SEEDS

Planting seeds in darkness
and in the depths of night
Are left in faith that one day soon
their shoots will see the light
Trusting in the darkest hour
the seed knows what it takes to flower
As springtime's flower ends its days
the seeds of its rebirth it lays

We plant the seeds of intentions and motivations in dark places – the void, stillness. Our deepest intentions are the work of our souls. They have a quality of purpose to them that allows us to trust that they will be supported and nurtured to fruition.

Even in the depths of winter when all appears still, there is potential lying dormant, waiting for the conditions to change. The same is true of us, that in dark moments of doubt, our deepest intentions are still within and will one day flower. From small projects to the work of a lifetime, a continuous cycle of intentions and then creating supportive conditions is how we grow and encourage our flowers to bloom. It is as if the universe conspires to help us bring our dreams and deepest intentions to life by nudging us in the right direction by bringing the right help, situations, and learning opportunities to us.

From another perspective, trees just grow and flower depending on the seeds and conditions. They just do. There is no existential crisis, no wondering about timing. They are just flourishing according to their nature. It is in them all along.

What if we planted seeds of awakening in all beings? What if they were already there in all of us waiting for the right conditions? What if we could help create the conditions that support an upward spiral of nurture for everyone?

Flowering and rebirth are for all of us.

## ENDLESS RAIN

All my inner clouds have gone
but water still remains
falls as tears
becomes the waves
and so is drawn again
to rise once more into the skies
to fall as endless rain

There are endless cycles of birth, growth, death and regeneration. The obvious and the less obvious. From the things we readily see and relate to, to all the countless processes that are going on right now in our body, in our natural world and in society. Most of this we take for granted, or else it occurs far beneath our conscious mind or anywhere we can possibly place our limited attention.

Everything is in endless transformation from one condition to another. These changes can be sudden and dramatic, or very subtle. The causes and conditions that create and sustain a change are in themselves causes of future changes and conditions. Inner can become outer. Outer can become inner.

Inner clouds can become rain for flowers and great trees, the waves of mighty oceans, or drinking water for thirsty children.

## NO REASON

Out in the dunes under stars that glisten
So much to say but no one's listening
I could tell you that you are the earth, the starlight and the sky
Knowing that it all just is
No reason to ask why

When we look up at the night sky we are filled with a sense of wonder. Wonderment at the infinite nature of time and space which lies beyond the grasp of our minds – the vastness of it all is far beyond our comprehension. The billions of suns, their light and the consuming darkness. The millions of humans before us who too have gazed up in awe at the scale and mystery of the unknown.

But that is only what we can see. There are unseen worlds in, beyond, and around us that our cognition and reason cannot yet understand – but that have been a part of the human experience for thousands of years.

It is a wonder to rest peacefully in the knowledge that the universe is unfolding in its own way, that we are both insignificant and nothing – yet at the same time – a vital and important expression of its wholeness.

Trusting in a benevolent universe and forces beyond our ordinary perception can be hard, but in the vastness of time and space what else can we do?

We are far greater than we think.

Trust in yourself.

## DIAMONDS

If you could be what you really are
underneath your mind
If you could see beyond the stars
what else would you find?
Freedom that was always here
but somehow never seen
Love beyond your daily fears
is what you've always been

Time that never really ends
and never really starts
More than mind can comprehend
is what you really are
So trust your soul and don't ask why
its wisdom's unsurpassed
Diamonds searched for in the sky
are buried in your heart

We tend to look beyond ourselves and our daily reality in the search for who we really are and our quest for validation, meaning and purpose.

Real freedom is within. It is the freedom to be yourself, your true self: most loving, deeply in touch with your gifts and abilities, and able to draw on, grow and encourage wonderful qualities in yourself and others. Free to choose with an open heart. Free to connect to what is here at the deepest levels of our experience. Free to not follow the demands of others and the invitations of consumer capitalism. Free to live in connection to nature, and less through technology and media. Free to live in the moment without the restrictions we place on ourselves or those we acquire from others.

Especially to be free of our daily fears. The ones that tell us we are not enough, whether these are generated internally or externally. Our fears of death, failure, success, missing out, not being in control, being alone, our past, our future, our powerlessness, our power. Fear takes on so many different guises as the ego morphs from one form to another.

It is possible to simply find our heart in the present moment. As we find it more and more, moment to moment, we become an embodiment of our truth and find joy in our aliveness.

We learn to hear our heart wisdom, the part of us that is timeless, wise and true. We come to realise and feel the heart as a centre of consciousness and intelligence all of its own, one which goes far beyond the mind. This timeless space is where we find our true freedom.

As much as we search outside of ourselves for what we really are or want, or for things that will ease our experience and give us meaning, the real treasures are within. The diamonds are great acts of love, creation and the ability to rest deeply in ourselves as we truly are. They are the great qualities of being: kindness, compassion, joy and inclusiveness.

For ourselves. For all beings.

~
INSPIRATION

## JUST ONE BREATH

The breath of a monk before he speaks
his words of truth and loving speech
The music in the quietness of
a garden that is grown with love

*For Brother Phap Dung – Plum Village*

Loving speech and deep listening seem to be in short supply in our world – for both ourselves and others. We are increasingly living at a superficial level in many of our relationships, amidst the loud demands that compete for our attention. The ability to encourage loving speech towards ourselves is the foundation of self-compassion, and being our own support and advocate helps us to navigate our anxieties. To find the same loving speech for others in an increasingly polarised world is both a means of bridging the gap by building shared understanding and greater tolerance, and is also a positive way forward for humanity.

The same is true of deep listening. Only by listening deeply to ourselves and others do we come to understand what our deepest needs are and to have empathy, not just for ourselves but for our shared human condition.

The first thing we give another is our presence. We feel it in others before we have even spoken. It is possible to grow and develop our loving essence in a place of great compassion and understanding. It shows how much heartful work has been done to arrive at a place of insight, transformation and wisdom.

Some people are an embodiment of great presence, wisdom, love and compassion. These qualities shine through, amplifying their natural talents and abilities. I've been fortunate to meet some beautiful souls and learn from them. They have all had great teachers and no doubt would be the first to acknowledge that it is those teachers who have allowed, recognised and cultivated those qualities within them. This is how true wisdom has passed down through the ages and withstands the assault of those who claim exclusive access to it, and voices that distract us from it.

My heart has been touched by the wisdom and presence of one breath in and out. A breath that says everything about the true nature of us all. The silence in it can feel like a symphony in that single breath. All the love, teaching and wisdom that can be seen, heard and felt in one moment is beautiful.

The wise words are the music but the heart is the garden.

## WALK THE EARTH

If all could walk the Earth like you
and practice love in all we do
the world would be a kinder place
reflected in each smiling face

An embodiment of love in action.

We know it when we see it. We know it when we are it.

The invitation is to be it. Your own unique version of it.

Not your mind's idea of it, but your heart's expression.

## ONLY LOVE

You don't know now but will one day
When it comes you cannot say
Life becomes a living prayer
Only love will take you there

To live our lives day-to-day from a place of love and kindness connects us more fully to what we want to see in the world. By living our truth we change the world. It doesn't need to be for an external deity.

It is for your own true nature and that of all beings.

## UNDIVIDED

I ask for love to take my hand
guide me to its promised land
where all the things I've ever seen
now seem more radiant and serene
A depth to life is here right now
those with eyes to see know how
All the realms that we dismiss
are now all much more real than this
Our dream in which we're found is lost
and clearer when we know the cost
of our great divided hearts
which weren't divided at the start
The undivided bring peace to bear
and back to love will lead us there

We start our lives with no sense of division, no boundaries to our experience. Then we build them up. Barriers of all kinds. Physical, emotional, mental, spiritual.

We live in systems, cultures and nations that reinforce this sense of separation and an over-identification with form and structure, self and other. This is often at the expense of our sense of being, our humanity and our open-heartedness. A heart with no division sees existence as a whole with many parts. No separation. Ultimate diversity in a single unitive consciousness.

No division means perceiving everything as one. Everything. Every experience, every person, every being, every community, every realm.

Peace is not divided. Minds create division. Love creates unity. It is here now.

## BRIGHTER ROOMS

Take this gentle soul with thee
guide me to eternity
to dwell in hearts of mortal men
to fill with love, inspire and then
to dance again in brighter rooms
serve greater truths and someday soon
turn on the lights for all to see
a greater love, infinity

Humanity is on a journey towards wholeness and love, peace and reconciliation, harmony and equity.

The first step is the recognition that we are all one. Not just as human beings, but as part of something far greater. We are one and remain interconnected as families, communities, organisations, workplaces, governments, nations, ecosystems, the Earth, the cosmos.

What if that realisation were possible for everyone? How would we behave, and what would our world look like if this belief were more than just a possibility? What if it were alive in everyone? If we could inspire others towards this understanding and way of being through our own acts of being?

If oneness is the eternal truth of who we are, and living closer and closer to this truth is what we are meant to learn and do?

Imagine.

~

LIGHT UP THE WORLD

## THE FORGOTTEN WORLD

The forgotten world it sits and waits
locked outside the gilded gates
while the wealthy with the power
waste every single passing hour
growing ever greater wealth
at the cost of our collective health
fiddling while the planet burns
past the point of no return
Who watch the sick and dying
and hide behind their lying
words that obfuscate and spin
into virtue moral sin
and pass off greed as something strong
no more right and no more wrong
for as their greater profits grow
so do hearts of those that know
that in the end enough's enough
and now's a time to lead with love

The inequality in the world is greater than ever. Wealth and material riches beyond comprehension for some and poverty, disease and displacement for others. Everything else in between. The gap separating the richest from the poorest in the world is wider than it has ever been, and it is growing.

Millions of people in developing countries are starving and lack access to water or basic sanitation. A billion children live in poverty. Over sixty-five million are displaced by war and conflict. Disease affects billions in both developed and developing countries.

Climate change is one of the biggest threats to our existence but 'business as usual' and powerful vested interests are holding back progress by denying its existence and failing to address it.

Meanwhile, many of our leaders make political decisions based on personalities and parties rather than visionary policies and wise leadership. Existing political systems are failing to meet the needs of populations and of a world affected by transnational influences and our own destructive behaviours. The vulnerable are suffering the most, while the wealthy grow richer in the process.

The most powerful nations, leaders and corporations – with a few notable exceptions – are contributing to the world's problems instead of helping to ease them. Hamstrung by a lack of willingness and current systems that suppress the ability to create peace and sustainable change, we are stumbling along slowly in a paradigm that is failing. At the same time the Earth and future generations are crying out for radical change that will facilitate a greater shared understanding and a wiser course of action.

Fear, greed and conflict are not our natural state and yet they dominate the daily way of being and mode of operating for most of our leaders. Their primary focus is not on humanity and leading it to wholeness, equity and wellbeing. Our world leaders spend more time talking about economies, geopolitical power, party politics and profits instead of leading with genuine vision. The voices advocating for our collective humanity and the voices of those in the greatest need go unheard.

Much of the international media is owned by, and fawns over, the powerful who are preoccupied with trying to hold together broken systems, making and hoarding vast material wealth, rather than supporting a sustainable and positive vision for humanity. Content that adds to our dialogues of fear and serves the interests of large corporations is keeping the global population compliant, anxious and limited. From advertising to propaganda and political spin, words are used and abused to hide or avoid truths, or command our attention.

Around the world there is a relentless oversimplification and distraction from what is being played out at the highest levels of corporations and national governments. Most of our leaders are disregarding our current and future wellbeing – our human survival and the needs of future generations – instead consumed by extravagant short-term gains that can be made from exploiting human suffering and engaging in ecological destruction.

Morality seems to have disappeared from too many of our leaders' awareness and is conspicuously absent from much of our public debate. It is wrong to make vast sums of money from the killing and ill health of other beings. It is wrong to destroy the natural and social capital on which human societies and ecosystems rely. It is right to feed the poor and hungry, to provide them with safety, shelter, sanitation and access to clean water. It is right to provide healthcare and education to all.

What if our leaders matched and outshone their political and economic power with a love of humanity? They have the capacity to transform themselves and the world for good, yet, the magnitude of that ability and its potential goes unstated and unrealised. Some of the world's brightest minds are wasted on keeping unhelpful systems in place, instead of leading us into an age of harmony, equity and unity.

Fortunately, the world is waking up. We know it is possible to change because the capacity exists in all of us and there are many wonderful examples of wise, kind, inclusive and strong leadership to show us the way. They deserve more of our attention and we can learn from them that we have the heart, ingenuity, vision and means to make profound changes to the wellbeing of everyone on the planet. We can create the right conditions for the relief of suffering, true sustainability and a healthier world in balance.

There is a big trick to watch out for though. It's one that says 'my heart is purer or better than yours', it is a distortion and a co-opting by the mind of our true intentions and ways of the heart. It is a similar trick to the one corporations and governments use when they use the language of the heart to manipulate. They are adopting uplifting words but operating from a different intention. We need to see through this and look at their motivations and our own, which are obvious if we can only pause and learn to see them clearly.

We can become more content and peaceful by tuning in to the sources of a deeper and more genuine happiness that is available now in this moment. Our daily choices and behaviours can help to support a more integrated way of being on all levels of our being. Abundance, contentment and the equitable sharing of resources is a healthier and more sustainable basis for action.

True leadership is of the heart. All our truly great leaders have been an embodiment of this. In the course of human history, no one will remember the corporate executives, politicians and world leaders who destroy humanity and the environment. They will remember those who raised our collective consciousness and protected the Earth and humanity, those who helped to end suffering, inequity and injustice.

Real heart-based leadership doesn't need to manipulate. It just strongly, steadily and lovingly does its work from a place of knowing. It calls out injustice and uses resources and positions of influence for good. Modesty and humility are the hallmarks of great leaders who know their purpose. They are also strong in their authentic power. You can see it in their words, their actions and their being. You can feel it. It is not separation, it is an invitation to something greater than we are.

We surely need those of great intellect, knowledge and understanding but their abilities need to be filtered through the lens of the heart. Otherwise our knowledge too easily becomes a complex mountain of information when what we urgently need is applied wisdom.

Courageous leaders operate primarily from their heart. They know they are not separate from those they represent. They care for nature, communities, organisations and others as if they were that. They know they are that.

The change we need is at the level of consciousness, vision, heart and embodiment.

It is time to lead with love.

# A CHANGE OF HEART

Time for change, a change of heart
Before the world gets torn apart
by leaders who think they're doing good
While those who starve and want for food
fear and hurt while greater deeds
remain undone by those who lead
While harm to our environment
is sanctioned by our governments
Freedom and democracy
a sham for those too blind to see
Free to live and free to choose
to please consume and drink the news
Oceans cleared for little food
forests felled but just for wood
warn us of the days to come
If we don't change and see the world
As ours on loan not to be sold
Is it too late? we ask ourselves
To look inside, find inner wealth
New leaders who will care enough
Great deeds are done by those who love

As much as we can develop and encourage inner change, ultimately it finds its expression in the outer world.

Our leaders, who might express high ideals, spend most of their time working within a very narrow range of vision. They have been subsumed into larger systems that do not have our collective human and environmental needs as their priorities.

Environmental regulations and protections are being routinely watered-down and disregarded. Nature continues to be brought into private ownership, from forests and oceans, to mineral deposits and biological processes. They are our common wealth and our common health depends on their integrity and longevity.

Democracy is held up as the overriding virtuous system of government of our time. It is certainly a better model than despotic dictatorships, sham governments and autocracies. However, what we call democracy is a long way from its stated ideals or how we like to think of it with its guiding principles of human rights, liberty, equality, fairness and representation for all.

In most democracies, every few years or so we have a 'choice' to elect from a narrow field of preselected candidates offering one of two views. Most votes have little bearing on the final result due to constituency boundaries and two-party systems. Candidates that win elections are predominantly those with supportive donors and connections to existing political structures and party systems.

It is more accurate to call western democracy an economic oligarchy. Politicians, voting systems, corporate and vested interests, and a bewilderingly limited lack of vision offer little choice to voters – let alone provide an inspiring and constructive way forward for us all.

Most of our leaders don't speak their truth, they say what they are told to say and manage their appearances and responses to deliberately avoid scrutiny and accountability. Political and corporate messaging is designed to avoid questions and deeper investigation, and to take our attention to carefully crafted points of view often far removed from the truth. It is obvious that they are not speaking from the heart.

Power and influence are bought and policies do not reflect the wishes of the majority of populations. That's in democracies. In other systems speaking your truth can be a life-threatening choice. Even peaceful critics are silenced, sometimes brutally so.

Entire populations are controlled, dumbed down and suppressed. Some very obviously, some more subtly. Television, endless frivolous entertainment, news cycles and shopping keep populations in fear and trapped in excessive consumerism rather than being truly free, empowered and uplifted.

When our leaders talk about freedom they are no longer talking about true freedom. They are referring to the freedom to be controlled to a point where we have such little autonomy over our bodies and minds that we spend most of our days meeting the needs of others and those needs we have had created within us that constantly need to be fed or sold to. This is not true freedom. It is freedom within a collective prison. Most of the media helps to define and reinforce the walls.

We are using the world's agricultural land and water resources with reckless inefficiency and with disastrous consequences for the health of ecosystems, biodiversity, topsoil, human health and animal welfare. The environmental and health impacts of land clearing, industrial fishing and eating meat are massive. Rainforests and oceans are being cleared at an alarming rate. Land is being used for animal feed and grazing, rather than to feed healthy soils and starving humans. Most industrial fishing is bycatch. Ocean ecosystems are in collapse. Billions of animal lives are taken every year. Sadly, the diversity and scale of impact on health, welfare and the environment are beyond most of our comprehension or awareness. Our behaviours would be vastly different if we truly knew and understood.

We are tearing the Earth apart at an unprecedented rate with complete disregard for the future. The oceans and forests are our life support system. We are dismantling them.

We are blithely continuing on with our rapacious consumption with barely a thought for the long-term consequences. Our dominant behaviours and way of being are completely unsustainable and the growing uptake of the same values and expectations in developing countries with massive populations will only add to the scale of the problem. Our survival as a species is at stake.

Stewardship is a core value of indigenous traditions. It means looking after resources for future generations. When we lived in smaller communities we knew we had to protect, respect and care for our resources in order to survive and maintain the natural balance into the future. We can encourage each other to scale-up that understanding to the collective on an enormous scale, and quickly, even in the face of powerful vested interests. For our own sake and for future generations, we should make the most sustainable and healthy choices we possibly can now. This means a very significant shift to what most of us regard as necessary and important. We can consume much less and redefine what we really need and want. At the same time we can better understand the impact of what we do and the decisions we choose to take.

We can also encourage new sustainable ways of being and the integration of systems. We can ask what is good for our body, mind, spirit, community, environment, Earth, and future generations. They are mutually reinforcing and life-giving. What supports one can support all.

Material consumption, greed, violence, inequality and environmental destruction can be overcome. Kindness, peace, sustainability, poverty reduction, human wellbeing and environmental restoration are more important in rebalancing our world. We can build an economy in service to these greater aims. Policies and systems that create the conditions that restore and rebuild us and return us to wholeness will be essential. 'Business as usual' is not working.

A progressive agenda based on equality and equity is urgently needed as a counterbalance and way forward. Non-violence and inclusiveness are core requirements in pursuing the practical means of changing our current practices and existing systems of business and government.

Part of the solution is to offer better alternatives, passionately advocate for them and maintain firm opposition to systems and groups who are not serving the greater good. Collaboration, vision and some honesty about intentions are essential. We can encourage new models of leadership and new leaders who are able to see from a vastly wider perspective and offer vision and collaboration for all.

Our world is in urgent need of more heart-centred leaders. Embodiments of loving action. We need them everywhere and at every level of our global community. Our great leaders are those who show us our common humanity. Our loving capacity to live in harmony and unity with the Earth and each other. They know it in themselves first.

Real change happens on the level of consciousness. Within our leaders and especially within our future leaders. Heart-centred education and wisdom for all are essential.

## SLEEPING GIANTS

No one really noticed when she stepped into the room
They were all too busy talking about the economic boom
Who would ever notice there's a giant to behold?
With hearts as closed as blinded eyes fixated on the gold

She spoke up very loudly, "there's a sleeping giant in here!"
Her voice went by unnoticed in the corporate atmosphere
Who would see a giant with their eyes turned to the world?
Greed and anger all abound, abusive words are hurled

We all have sleeping giants waiting to awake
The only question left to ask, is how long will it take?
For someone to stand in the dark and bring the world to light
In boardrooms, nations and ourselves, find peaceful loving quiet

For in the quiet we find our giant is always here to stay
Our mind so busy running that we chase our giant away
And when we're still amidst the noise and rage of inner storms
Our giant takes care of all with love and tender caring warmth

Though we spend our precious time waiting to begin
Fighting fear and darkened thoughts that keep us locked within
Our sleeping giants lie in our hearts and come to seize the day
When love will win, it never lost and can't be held at bay

What if all the world were giants and living from their heart?
A new day dawned, begin anew, humanity to start
No divide of them and us, no more me and you
Come to love and wake your giant, your giant lives in you

More feminine leadership would be a great help to us all, irrespective of gender. This is true of us internally and both within organisations and at all levels of our global society.

Corporate environments and political agendas are for the most part driven by profit, competition and ego. There is an enormous opportunity for more feminine qualities to be consciously cultivated to create balance and sustainable futures for all.

Economics and economic measures are devoid of a meaningful assessment of the true value of natural resources or human potential. The current economic model is not serving us well. It is failing the poorest and it is failing the planet. Until we change our perspective to see economic models as the servant of humanity rather than its master, we are destined to diminish nature and our wellbeing with potentially catastrophic circumstances.

Businesses and governments should be supporting and growing humanity and nature, not the other way around. We can do business differently. It is possible to reorient the values and systems of business to better serve us. The reorientation starts with vastly greater vision and a much broader and integrated perspective of who we are, our relationship to each other and the natural world.

Greater compassion, empathy, inclusiveness and care are inspiring to see in the world and especially in governments, corporations and large organisations. Leadership with greater balance is possible and there are many wonderful voices and examples to listen to and support. Our sense of purpose and destiny depend on where we place our attention and the qualities we can bring forth. This is true in our own personal sense of leadership and also in the leaders we choose to support.

The wisdom to see the full scope and impact of decisions that are adversely affecting the way we live and the future we are leaving for coming generations is the next great step forward.

Heart-centred leaders will change the world.

Wake your giant.

## A SILENT CALL

A call to action, gentle arms
A call for love in all its forms
A call for peace in all the world
In every boy, in every girl
In every single living thing
A joyful heart, a song to sing
A doorway to the other side
Where love is known and never hides
Where the only constant sound's
A silent peace that knows no bounds

Peace in the world starts within.

Violence comes from misunderstanding. Kind, loving action towards peace grounded in the principle of non-violence is a noble and achievable aim.

Conflict, violence, displacement and trauma have a powerful effect on people, and the flow-on impacts on families, societies and cultures can last for generations. Making peace with ourselves, self-forgiveness and the forgiveness of others are important foundations for helping to end conflict.

We don't achieve greater peace through entrenched opposition and escalation but through understanding and a commitment to our shared humanity. We support it by recognising that the suffering of conflict is often the same for both sides and asking what are the causes and conditions for peace and how they can be created. Respect, a fair allocation of resources and greater equity go a long way in building shared understanding, peaceful intentions and goodwill.

Our world leaders would be wise to work towards peace and understanding through commitment and example. Peaceful intentions and actions will lead to peace. Time, money and resources spent on escalating conflict would be better spent in creating the conditions for lasting harmony and reconciliation. Asking for, and supporting leaders who can create and grow peace in themselves and their communities is possible. Many fine examples exist across all traditions and cultures. We can listen to their wise words and encourage them to the highest levels.

Ultimately, peace starts with learning to find and grow it

within and then teaching others the same ability – especially our children.

The shared truth of all traditions is a starting point, as is our own breath.

Peace is what we are.

## ALL THE SAME

You are the essence of your religion not the violence in its name
You are the heart of each tradition – love and kindness all the same

The violence done in the name of religion is one of the greatest misunderstandings we have made as a species. Millions of lives lost, violence, subjugation, abuse of power, appropriation of resources, division of communities, intergenerational trauma, destruction of indigenous cultures, and more have all happened on a massive scale.

Love, kindness and unity are at the heart of every tradition. This is the common understanding to which they all point. Respect and care for ourselves, our bodies, minds, feelings, talents, abilities, nature, each other, and humanity are all present.

Ultimately all traditions point to unitive consciousness. The direct experience of it and the insight, understandings and behaviours that flow from that realisation. Everything is one.

The notion that 'my truth or tradition is more valid or important than yours' takes us towards separation and away from understanding. It takes us towards conflict and away from peace. We have been heading down this path for too long.

Learning respect for the essence of all spiritual traditions is important. To recognise that the external face is just a face, that cultural traditions and practices have their place but they can talk to each other as well, is a much-needed bridge towards lasting peace. There are many beautiful examples of interfaith dialogue, support, understanding, generosity and reconciliation. They are all built on the deeper truth that we are each other.

Many great traditions of all cultures have beautiful elements and honouring them is respectful, and can be a beautiful practice and source of true community. Recognising their diversity, inherent value and wisdom is a source of learning for all of us.

Becoming attached to the dogma or the external appearances, without being connected to their essential qualities and wisdom as a lived experience, is to miss the beauty and fullness of them.

When they become an unattainable vision or an externalised set of ideas that mean access to any sense of personal or transpersonal divinity has to be mediated solely through a church, a place of worship, a priest, a cleric, a guru, then we move further away from our own truth and the essential truth which they share.

Wise teachers of any tradition point us towards the eternal truth irrespective of the person or the setting. Their compassionate and loving hearts can be transformative examples at the deepest levels of our being and contact with teachers who are established in the truth of their essential nature can light up our own being, sometimes in the most profound ways.

Divinity within and the divine which permeates all existence is an expression of love and kindness.

## RETURN OF THE KING

Home to what you've always been
Warrior King of the unseen
Walk both worlds below above
Gifts to light the world with love

Dive into the great unknown
The greatest love unseen is shown
Moving on from lost truth-seeker
In your soul a wisdom keeper

You know the truth was always here
Underneath the doubt and fear
And in your corner of the world
Your flag to love has been unfurled

The mighty army you will lead
Fights with arms and hearts of peace
The world will change for all to see
Love for all humanity

A peaceful revolution starts
With loving, strong and gentle hearts
Strength to change the human plight
A heart to bring the world to light

Your peaceful warrior stands beside you
Your inner wisdom helps and guides you
All the things you've ever been
Are here to live, now to be seen

Those for love and unity
Peace, respect and harmony
With words and actions cast from light
Will long outshine this darkest night

These broken times are not the end
Begin again our world defend
Death will always lead to birth
A new respect for Mother Earth

A kinder world of which we're part
Lives in every human heart
So claim it back, what matters most
From those whose power love is lost

Live in love and lead us on
Peace inside the battle's won
In each of us and all as one
Live in love, it will be done

We all have inner warrior kings and queens of loving-kindness and compassion. Embodiments of strength and ardency, wisdom and authentic power. In touch with the physical world in which we live and the divine qualities of being. At the same time, deeply connected to a greater sense of self and spirit, in touch with the numinous.

Over the last few thousand years, we have created some distorted ideas of what it means to be a man. Conquest, domination and subjugation feature prominently. Our collective has created images of successful men as materially wealthy, physically dominating and exercising power over others – especially women. By furthering the current model and archetype, we are creating the conditions for disintegration, subservience, separation and dominance, and will perpetuate systems and societies that continue inequality. At the same time, we can recognise that much of this behaviour and way of being is the result of many causes and conditions, intergenerational conditioning and societal norms that go unaddressed and belong to a bygone era.

Our societies are increasingly comprised of men who have not grown into their maturity, their fullness. It has become too easy, and the demands of society so great, to reach a position of status and material wealth and to stop growing as a person. Wealth beyond a certain point does little for our highest self unless we use it to do good in the world. Many men have become cut off from their bodies and souls and turn away from their development, their inner journey and what that could mean for the future.

We could help ourselves by calling back what it really means to be a man. A more divine version of the masculine as living examples of what that can look like and the positive effect it can have on all males. More loving fathers, sons and brothers would help us all. To also support these qualities in women as part of a change in consciousness that asks us to live more lovingly and in a more integrated way.

The world would benefit from the restoration of a more balanced version of the masculine principle. These beautiful attributes are an inherent part of our being, whether male or female. The ability to create safety, support and protection, care, opportunity, and empowerment for all. Confident, firm and active. Rational without being arrogant, rigid or overly cerebral. In full possession of a developed intellect, in service of the heart, and operating for the good of others. Abundant without being greedy. Equitably sharing and ensuring wise stewardship of resources. Straight talking and honest with insight, ideas and right actions. These great gifts help us to illuminate our talents and encourage the same attributes in others. It is a divine masculine which supports, co-exists with, and uplifts a divine feminine in a mutually enhancing exchange. Internally, externally and collectively.

Most of our leaders are not great men. They are grown-up adolescents and young men with great power and wealth at their disposal. We would benefit from more leaders who have grown into their elderhood. Wise, loving and truthful for all of those whom they are responsible. Truly visionary and able to lead and make decisions that benefit future generations.

We can recast ideas of leadership so that it can be heart-driven without throwing out the intellect. We truly need some powerful intellects, policy makers and conscious leaders that are able to take in a broader scope to decisions. The systems of our interconnected world are so complex and far-reaching, that we will need both greater vision and greater wisdom to allow us to bring forward the solutions we need.

We also need to redefine what it means to be a male leader as standing fully in possession of their true masculine power, not the distorted ideas which currently dominate the landscape. We would be well-served by men to stand up for a better ideal of manhood and its possibilities, including respect for the feminine within, for women, and for Mother Earth. We need much more divine feminine leadership too.

Imagine leaders who can hold the whole of humanity in their consciousness and embrace values that are supportive of all. Those who can call up their masculine and feminine strengths, regardless of gender and the roles they play, will help us find our way back to wise wholeness.

A vision of a greater humanity needs new leaders to bring it into being. A new way of being that is grounded in compassion and with the higher mind in service to the heart and the greater good. We can educate, choose, and empower future leaders who can live and act from this place without getting lost in the material attractions and intoxicating abuse of power.

The 'reason versus spirit' argument has become an unhelpful polarised debate. We have spent a lot of time and energy on an apparent choice which is not really a choice. It is a misunderstanding. We can encourage and choose heart-based leaders who can see the interconnected nature of things and who can use and develop their skills, talents, and emotional and intellectual intelligence for the good of humanity. Embodiments of loving-kindness and wisdom, using their power courageously and for good, who can create peace and the conditions for peace from loving strength.

We can all stand as a peaceful warrior for love in all its forms. The banner of love unfurled; the swords of intellect and compassion to cut through the unhelpful inner and shared stories; a protective shield of kindness for the vulnerable to hold back aggressors who seek to harm those who work towards peace, understanding and kindness. Imagine armies of peaceful warriors, not rising in anger but in authentic power and inclusiveness, steadily doing their work for humanity and the Earth. Speaking words of powerful truth, benevolence and influence. Living in love and peace, making decisions and taking action from that place within; stronger than anything.

The starting point is to come to peace within. To learn how to be with difficult emotions and situations, and to regulate and calm our being. To speak and act wisely from the heart. To not fight the unnecessary battles within, as by fighting we contribute to the very forces we seek to overcome. To not identify too much with our peaceful warrior king or queen but to be it. To recognise that we have all the wonderful capacities we need in ourselves now and to grow them and live them out. We can meet the greatest challenges with love.

In the end we must all answer the question, What do we stand for?
Really. At our core and after all the superficialities have been stripped away. What do we stand for?

I'm for love.

Truly, love conquers all.

## MY WAKING WORLD

She was my love, my waking world
My open-hearted wide-eyed girl
The one for which I lived my life
The gift I gave my loving wife

She was the wisdom of the ages
Her smile the love of ancient sages
Her mother, keeper of the Earth
Her father, witness to new birth

Taken then by unfair means
And left behind her anguished screams
Which filled me up with grief and rage
My dreams locked up, my heart a cage

My lives and journeys fell through time
Just shadows of a life divine
She was the future, all of me
My greatest love, my legacy

I lost myself without her love
Her hand to hold was just enough
Her shining eyes looked right through me
Into my soul, eternity

Nothing left for me to give
I'd given up the will to live
I jumped into the funeral pyre
I myself became the fire

Armies killed in dark revenge
My bloodied hands her soul avenged
The earth aflame with broken hearts
I broke the entire world apart

My love replaced with heavy chains
My care with anger, guilt and shame
'Til only broken hearts remained
Death and destruction I became

One still day I heard her voice
Amongst the chaos and the noise
"Light up the world I never died,
Love in all can never hide."

Remember now how she lives on
Inside of me, in everyone
A loving smile your beautiful girl
Her heart the centre of the world

As she was gone so now my grief
My soul at last has come to peace
Now I look into all eyes
And see the love that never dies

There may be nothing as innocent and beautiful, living in joy and wonderment, as a little girl. Her infinite creative potential a source of life in the world. An empowered woman to be – deeply connected to the needs of the Earth, children, community and future generations. To grow into a divine feminine fullness and an expression of love and wisdom.

We all know that open-hearted creative innocence. It has a billion faces and countless manifestations. She is the creative principle in all things.

While we all have these forces in ourselves, we tend to deny the divine feminine – our creativity, nurture and intuition – in the face of an excessively hard masculine rationality.

Deeper than that, we have subjugated and destroyed the feminine in the collective for the last two thousand years and more. Religions and doctrines that have denied the power or the equal rights of women both in society and organisationally have denied the fullness of the feminine. At the same time, they have diminished the true masculine.

Disempowering, discriminating against and destroying the feminine is a distorted masculine which further distorts each time it subjugates the feminine. Men would be better served and wiser to call back the feminine in themselves and honour it in women rather than subjugate, dominate or distort it.

Every time we kill, diminish, or subjugate another we are doing the same to that aspect of ourselves. This can be at a soul level. The effect this pain, this denial and destruction has on our humanity is massive. Communities have been destroyed, cultures decimated, nature and our common wealth plundered.

The effects of trauma are passed from one generation to the next leaving trails of suffering down the ages in our collective. The impact of losing a child on our being is so great and affects us deeply on many levels.

Intergenerationally, we have spent thousands of years destroying the Earth, our children, mothers and daughters. As the source of life to new generations, empowering women to reach their greatness should be our goal.

Our Great Mother is the Earth. Every cell in our body comes from her and will return to her. When we live out of harmony with her we create disharmony in ourselves. She will live on long after we are gone as a species. We have a choice in how long we are here with her and the conditions in which we will live.

The feminine principle is beautiful. From the innocence of children to the wonder of creation; from birth and nurture, to deep intuition and psychic knowing; from patience and joy, to flexibility and healing. These are all aspects of the divine feminine to find and honour in ourselves and others, regardless of gender.

Imagine what it might be to embody the divine feminine and not the distorted ideas our patriarchal society has set up of that. Women everywhere fully in their power and choice, not a male prescribed idea of it. This is true female empowerment. Not to be the distorted masculine version, but fully feminine balanced with their own inner divine masculine.

Beyond that exists the possibility of female/male partner-ships that are the recognition of the fullness of both in their divine aspects, and that mutually support each other to reach their individual and shared potential. This is also possible in our collective. It is the way forward for the masculine in us and our collective to honour our own feminine and masculine attributes. Balance within and balance without. An expression of the truth of the interaction of the female and male principles, the play of yin and yang.

The Earth and all beings are in great need of empowered feminine leadership. Collectively we need more of the feminine to bring us back to balance. Greater kindness and nurture would benefit all of us everywhere.

To look at someone deeply and see the creative principle in them is a wonder. Everything that has come together for this one unique expression of consciousness itself. The same is true of nature and the miracle of existence itself. The divine feminine is girls and women of all ages, backgrounds and cultures; Mother Earth, the feminine and creative principle itself in everything. She is beautiful.

She is the void from which all creation comes. We could destroy everything and something would still issue forth from her.

The true feminine is indestructible. She lives in all of us.

The light of the world.

## THE EAGLE

My highest self got hurt so much it left and flew away
Safe upon its mountain peak it always liked to stay
Its clearest view kept watch from high to guide the rest of me
To life lived with an open heart and vulnerability

The part of me that stayed behind was lost or so it seemed
Without its inner guidance my head was full of dreams
Bodies with no compass and no light to find the way
Stumbled through the darkness until the dawn of day

Fighting off the demons who chased my love away
Who killed me on that far-off land and took my child to slay
Who broke the line of wisdom with the tyranny of violence
While angels came to save me with their song of loving silence

It kept still watch for lifetimes while I learned to feel my power
Return again and learn until I found my finest hour
To call it back into myself and come down from above
It never really left me and its cause is endless love

My eagle's up there watching from its highest mountain peak
It calls to me with courage when my heart begins to speak
For those who just like me were lost when love had flown away
But now my love's inside of me this time it's back to stay

We all have inner eagles though the demons are still here
Breaking our connection with their wars and words of fear
Killing off our mother, how dare they use God's name
It's just a different era but the Earth is still the same

For all of those whose souls took flight in that far-off land
I did everything I could, I was the last to stand
We lived in love and harmony with all of life on Earth
And will return to show the way, humanity's rebirth

Too much time spent waiting and living out the past
Unfurled wings must feel the winds of love to lift at last
Cloudless is the eagle's view in wisdom's clear blue sky
Soaring from the highest peak, love is meant to fly

Deep within our hearts is a knowing of what we are meant to do, of what lifts us up and inspires us at the most fundamental level of who we are. It is what we love to do, what gives us joy and is our gift to humanity. We also know there is a part of us that acts for our highest good and the highest good of others. They do not have to be mutually exclusive.

The demands of social and familial conditioning, education, available opportunities, and the course of life itself can take us a long way from who we are and what we know we are born to do. Our personal truth can be deeply hidden out of fear of not wanting to show our true selves, our talents, our successes and our failures. We can also find ourselves on paths or living in situations and working in jobs that are far from our highest good, our deepest truth, or our greatest potential.

For some of us, traumatic experiences cause us to shut down or cut off parts of who we really are because at some level the expression of our true self was overwhelmed by this experience. This can be buried deep in our subconscious and we may not even be aware of it without help and determination to uncover it.

This is our soul purpose.

For me there has been much soul searching, self-inquiry, the meeting of some dark experiences and beginning a journey to touch what that is in me. Calling those hidden aspects of ourselves back is a gift, one which returns us to wholeness if we can see the lesson it contains and use it wisely. It is what shamans call 'soul retrieval'. To touch who we are in our heart and then to live our lives from that understanding is profound. If we can live from the deepest realisation of who and what we really are, we are able to transform our own being, our lives, and positively influence those around us.

At our essence we are here to love ourselves and each other, to bring our gifts to the world, and to support our own individual and collective awakening. The wellbeing of humanity and the planet depends on us finding and encouraging this in everyone.

We are also here to speak our truth with confidence and purpose, and to learn that words have great power when spoken from a place of insight. We can encourage more wise words and nurture great leaders, not of the angry and oppositional kind, but of a truth that shines brighter than the current accepted practices that define our world. Limitless growth, the inequitable use of our collective resources and a disregard for the environment and our species is not wise action.

We need to hear more of the voices of the voiceless. Those of the disempowered, the subjugated, the animals, the Earth, the marginalised and the forgotten. Especially the voices of those insightful and articulate enough to advocate for those who are unable. Words of truth, vision and love are in short supply, drowned out by those who fill our consciousness and experience with unhelpful messages and distractions. There is a great need for non-violence, powerful silence, love and spoken truth in the face of power and the abuse of it.

For the most part of our human evolution, we have lived in harmony with the planet and each other. Yes, there have and will be conflicts but the scale, rate and impact of this conflict, humanitarian suffering, species extinction, pollution, environ-mental degradation, biodiversity loss, and more – is greater than ever. This is particularly true of the last few thousand years. It is so significant and man-made that we are now well into the Anthropocene: an era that defines our relationship with the Earth as influenced by the activities of humans.

Indigenous traditions throughout the world recognise our deep connection to the Earth and the environment that supports us at every level of our being. This is more than just a logical, mind-based idea that we need to look after our environment, but a felt sense that we are the Earth – that the elements exist in us and that we live in a symbiotic relationship with the world around us. Beyond that is a connection to the unseen, that the spiritual has a manifest and unmanifest aspect. This understanding is a core feature of the spiritual traditions that pre-date and permeate the major religions of the world. The unbroken lineages of true wisdom that exist, and to which we owe much, are some of humanity's treasures.

The wise elders of those traditions understand this deeply and their life, culture and wisdom are oriented around the need to look after the environment upon which we depend for survival. Our modern world has broken the connection between our actions and the impacts they have on our local and global ecosystems. Decisions are made by governments, corporations, organisations, families, and all of us that do not take into account the true impact of our actions on ourselves, our families, our environment or our communities. Our physical, mental, emotional and spiritual health and the conditions for our wellbeing are being left out.

The reduction of nature and the growth of suffering in the

name of God is a profound misunderstanding. The idea that humans have nature as ours to do with what we will is an unhelpful perspective. In the same way, to invoke God while destroying nature is to miss the truth. It is the same distorted view that invokes a god while committing acts of harm and killing. The nature of divinity is unity. How can we kill or destroy something that *is* us? What we harm in the world we harm in ourselves.

It is possible to grow out of our misguided interpretations and reconnect to our deepest collective wisdom. Our personal power and gifts are needed in the loving service of our humanity and the Earth to ensure not just our survival as a species, but our way back to balance and our thriving.

Imagine we were all given that understanding and wisdom and could live our lives as our highest selves for our own joy, upliftment and flourishing as a means of service to humanity. What a community of beings, what a loving power and force for good in the world that would be. Alternate systems that properly represent the needs of all beings, and the environment and communities in which they exist, are essential.

I have spent a long time sitting on what I knew to be true in my heart. For all the times that I expressed it and was ridiculed as a dreamer or worse, I know in the depths of my heart that certain wisdom is universal and is meant to influence and guide us through the ages. Applying this wisdom to our current situations and making it relevant to our lives as they are is critically important when the wellbeing and future of our species are at risk.

Wise elders have been killed for their wisdom because their indigenous traditions didn't align with the desires of invading forces and their ideologies. We have so much to learn and restore about how to live in harmony with nature and with each other – from interfaith dialogues to learning about the deeper elements of who we are as a species, and our greatest human and spiritual potentials. All of these rest on the understanding that we are one. Not just one as a humanity, but one with everything.

It is possible to cultivate and grow the insight of 'interbeing', the understanding that nothing exists without the causes and conditions for it to exist, which themselves are brought into being by other phenomena. Everything 'inter-is' with everything else. At the same time, we have the capacity to influence those conditions in ourselves and in the collective. This understanding of 'interbeing' and the capacity to exercise our choice and free will are the basis from which we can remake and shape systems that allow for greater fairness, wellbeing – and beyond that – our flourishing.

I have also sat on my beautiful heart and stuffed down its wisdom, its truth and the truth of who I am at my deepest. It is only through feeling encouragement and upliftment that we allow our spirits to soar, our love to manifest in the world, and our gifts to flow.

The rebirth of humanity is not just a dream. It is our future. Compassion, peace, equity, inclusiveness, an end to suffering, are both the way forward and the destination. This means an end to poverty, restoration of the environment, and a commitment to re-ordering our world towards kindness. This is not in an unattainable conceptual way, but in a determined collective effort to align our actions with a greater vision and deeper understanding. We can remake ourselves, businesses, governments, societal structures and leadership to work better for all of us.

All of us have eagles deep within us. We need to call them back and spread our wings with clarity and wisdom.

We are all meant to fly.

## CHILDREN OF THE FUTURE

You children of the future
you elders of the past
definitely not the first
and surely not the last
Here before and come again
the seas, each wave a drop more rain
It keeps on falling and has no end
the endless ocean, the river bend
The time that stops is time to know
you are the eternal now
So keep it safe and hold with love
what lies below and climbs above
to see yourself in everything
in every breath, the out, the in
passing time as just a flow
seen by all and all who know.

To live in a way that is not just sustainable now, but will bring the Earth back to balance, is not just for our own children – but is for ourselves. We can encourage those who protect the Earth for future generations and have a heartfelt intention towards a kinder, more peaceful and thriving humanity.

We have to keep our planet safe, from the atmosphere and the oceans to the land and all of life on Earth. Stewardship of our shared resources for future generations is a core belief of many traditions. We can learn and remake our systems and behaviours based on that philosophy.

Greater love and compassion, and ways of thriving that are based on sharing the Earth's resources without diminishing them is the only way on a planet of finite resources. To live increasingly off the interest, and at the same time rebuild our natural, social, cultural and intellectual capital is essential.

By coming to understand that we are reliant on nature and the whole of existence for our own wellbeing, we can see we are all things. That we exist in everything that is, has ever been and will ever come to be. From understanding comes wise action. As our global elders have always known, what we do now affects our future.

We are the children of the future.

## A SPRING OF LOVE

An age that has been born of reason
is making way for a change of season
What we thought was summer has turned to fall
A spring of love now waits for all

For a long time we have been living in an era dominated by the outward manifestation of the rational mind. At the same time, important values have been disappearing from our public consciousness and certainly out of the daily awareness of our leaders.

The public exaltation of the intellect above the qualities and values that are closer to our heart is not helping us. The age of reason has given us many wonders, but we need to harness them for good. Reason driven by ego demands pushes us further into an unsustainable consumptive materialism. Balanced with love and wisdom, the intellect has the power to help bring forward a more just, more peaceful and more sustainable future for everyone. Where we place our attention is critical.

We are fast approaching an end to the age of reason, or at least the age that places intellectual reasoning above all other values. Values that are too easily omitted from our debate and decision making. Kindness and respect have fallen out of polity and business for the most part. Hard rationality and short-term thinking hold back a more creative, insightful and wise model of leadership.

Future generations will be living with the consequences of centuries of leadership based on physical, intellectual, military, and economic domination. It will be their task to bring the world back into balance. Providing true wisdom and insight to help them is the kindest thing we can do. This is especially true in an age of information and distraction that affects our abilities as humans to apply and discern what is valuable, not just in our own experience, but also for our collective wellbeing.

We can learn to come back to an embodied spirituality that recognises our connection to all of who we are on every level of our being. To turn our deepest knowing into action and influence in the world. To find our deepest insight and to live from there. To powerfully influence and shape the world and influence leadership towards the heart. It is the brightness of our light which we shine into the world which matters most.

Spirituality and rationality are not mutually exclusive. A new grounded and productive way forward for all of us depends on harnessing knowledge, filtering it through the heart, drawing on wisdom and putting action into the world that is of benefit to all beings.

The intellect can operate powerfully in service to the heart and with wisdom for the greater good. Only by expanding our circle of inclusiveness can we do this. We can and should consider ever-wider circles of concern and inclusion to make decisions from a higher vantage point. We can do this for all that we are as beings. Ultimately we must include all beings.

By leading with generosity of spirit, goodwill and love in action we can change the world for good.

We are not just our intellectual capacity, nor are we blind faith in religion. We are loving-kindness and respect for all beings.

Winter is nearly over.

A spring of love for humanity is coming.

~
LOVE AND BEYOND

## ALWAYS HERE

What is this that's always here
That stands alone without the fear
That sees the lives that come and go
Old to young each other flow
Silently watching all the thoughts
Knowing all will come to nought
Watching all this human drama
An end to all ideas of karma
Nothing that I think is me
Is left for even me to see
It's over now the search is done
Everything still here as one

If we look deeply we can see the rise and fall of birth and death in all things.

Our fear of death is writ large on our existence. Most humans tend to think we are limited to this life. It is a powerful collective story.

What if we are not limited to this body, this mind, this lifetime? How would we behave and what would the impact on our daily lives be? Not just superficially, but really. To truly sit with this possibility can be a little overwhelming, hence our resistance to look within, though it can also be a source of great comfort. More broadly, what if we were to come back to another human existence? What kind of world would we like to live in? How would we treat each other and the Earth?

We are the children of the future and elders of the past. When we create a better world for future generations, we are creating it for all of us – our continuations.

While searching for the ultimate truth of existence is beautiful and brings knowledge, ideas and insight, so too it can become poison. The inner journey can involve a lot of striving, but in the end it can just be more grasping for something else. We can find ourselves striving for non-striving. Trying to reach back to an experience or grasping for something in the future takes us further away from ourselves.

Karma and the endless cycles of cause and effect are big philosophical ideas that are true, but they can also be a dense forest in which we can easily get lost.

Eventually there is just the end of searching so hard and just being what you are, exactly as you are.

In stillness. All one.

## A BEAUTIFUL THIEF

All ideas are all the same
Then freedom from belief
A mystery gained by losing a name
Love is a beautiful thief

We live in a world of ideas and concepts. They take us away from our being, our deep being with each other, with nature, with our true nature.

They can limit our ability to experience life more deeply, exactly as it is, the suchness of the moment. To truly experience nature or another person or being as they are without all the labels and mind chatter. Even to meet the realities of our human experience exactly as they are, fully, and without unnecessary judgement.

Dropping labels and identities takes us from the mind into experience and beingness. It includes all the spiritual labels and beliefs as beautiful as they are. At some point, becoming too attached to them stops us fulfilling our personal truth or resting in the truth of who we really are.

Ideas and beliefs can take us to the edge but if we stay in our mind with them, we can only travel so far.

True love is beyond all concepts, ideas and beliefs.

## THE GREATEST LOVE

The greatest love I'll ever know doesn't make a sound
The sweetest kiss I'll ever taste is nowhere to be found
Call off the search and strain to hear there's nothing left to seek
The stillness that I find within sends tears down both my cheeks
The gentlest touch I'll ever feel is more than I can bear
The sleight of hand that lit the night is never far from here
So come again and let me know the wonder that is you
Because I want you so much but wanting isn't you

If grace comes, it is transformative. An experience of oneness has far-reaching consequences.

One taste of the truth sends our mind running after it with everything it has got. It is a wonder which we want more and more of, but the wanting is a trap. It is exhausting for our mind as the new sense of self busies itself trying to get back to some beautiful state which it cannot do. Grasping at the truth, and any of the wonder that goes with it, takes us further away from it.

That's not to say that spiritual practice isn't useful. It is. And it is important, beautiful and valuable on many levels, but if it becomes a new rod to beat ourselves with, or an impossible search, we are lost in our minds once more. Practices and wisdom that take us back to our heart and out of our mind are always beautiful and can help us break through. Holding everything lightly seems to be a useful way to continue on the journey.

The unrequited love of another or the divine can be a torment. It is both within reach, closer than we can imagine, and at the same time, untouchable.

The divine is in us all along but the grasping makes an idea of true love, one which our mind games turn into an unattainable perfection.

It is a surrender. Letting go more and more.

No more wanting.

## HERE RIGHT NOW

Give up the search and look again
Not still to come and hasn't been
It never was nor will it be
It's here right now for all to see

Awareness is here now.

It is unchanging. It doesn't go anywhere, so there is no need to be anywhere other than here, now. Fully present.

Our minds arising in awareness. Our body arising in awareness. Our experience arising in awareness.

Everything arising and passing in awareness.

Resting in awareness.

This eternal moment.

## ENDLESS SEA

I sat down and gazed upon a calm and endless sea
Sat 'til there was no one left, no, not even me

The thought of 'I' gets put in place quite early in life and it grows very strong as we assume and reinforce an identity. Everything then exists in relationship to our thoughts of who we are as an 'I' thought. My life, my experience, my emotions, my feelings, my body, my past, my future. These are an integral part of what it is to be human, and learning to care skilfully for them all is important to living our lives healthily and fully.

At the same time, there is the awareness of what we are before, during and after the identity of 'I'. Or rather, 'Who am I?'. This is the path of self-inquiry.

The divine is both transcendent and imminent. Existing and becoming. Our own highest-self being an expression of a greater Self. The Self that is no-self.

## LISTEN WELL

Listen well and it will come
The peace and quiet within the song
Stillness in activity
Action with serenity
Inner world anew begin
A peaceful heart
No out no in

Songs are both sound and silence. So too are our lives.

We can tune in to a deeper sense of ourselves and find quiet as we sing the songs of our lives.

Not thrown around so much by the ups and downs of daily life, or the demands of a busy inner dialogue, we can develop greater equanimity and steadiness as we create our own destiny. All the things we do in our lives are still there, but our quality of attention and engagement may differ. Our values and behaviours can change as we come to see what is truly important.

We can begin anew with our inner world at any time. We can do it in this moment, and we can do it daily. Great lives are built one day at a time on a foundation of love.

It is possible to live from our highest self with purpose, warmth, grace, kindness, strength, courage, humility, generosity, gratitude, abundance and compassion. We become an embodiment of these qualities and an inspiration to ourselves and others.

We come to express our soul and recognise our infinite nature.

A peaceful heart is our constant.

## NO MORE STORY

No more story left to tell
No more heaven
No more hell

Nothing left to do
Nothing left to be
Nowhere to go
Nowhere I've been

Nothing after
Nothing before
Nothing less
Nothing more

No path to tread
No way to find
No road ahead
No trail behind

No fear and nothing left to hold
Pure divine no love untold

We tell ourselves lots of stories. They tend to go with our labels and judgements of ourselves and of others. We can lose ourselves in them quite easily. I certainly have done.

Some stories are so great they influence entire populations. Our ideas of heaven and hell, alternate futures dependent on our behaviour and sometimes our servitude to false ideals, can be unhelpful. Our personal ideas of perfection and redemption lead us into fantasies of what we think we should be which are not always accurate or supportive. Even stories of spirituality and seeking can easily become new identities and stories of who we think we are. They can be endless loops that keep us away from ourselves.

It is helpful to come to a way of being where nothing is held too tightly. Ideas, memories and future plans can be more beautiful when held with a greater lightness.

We can allow space for all things to drop away and find a state of simply being. Not searching into the future, nor dwelling in the past. Not demanding more or less. Just being.

Underneath it we may find our presence. Standing fully in what we are at our deepest. Our most loving version of who we are – our Highest Self. In this space, we all have a story but we are no longer defined by it. It is an unfolding. We give ourselves more fully to it and let go at the same time.

Ultimately all holdings are released. All fears are seen to be transient and empty, as real as we think and feel them to be.

At last to speak of love, our own truth, universal truth. We don't always need words.

## THE CATCHING HAND

I'm standing on the edge of mind
about to make the leap
When I jump I know I'll find
There's nothing left to seek

I let go of the world of plenty
but know I'll never fall
The catching hand is empty
and I am love in all

At some point we might get to the edge of thoughts. It might be in meditation, whether sitting or moving. We might be so fully alive in a moment that our sense of self is absorbed fully into the doing. This is by moving through and beyond flow states into pure being. It is possible to lose sight of who we think we are and break through into undifferentiated beingness. Love in all might show itself.

From the mind's perspective, it's a lot easier said than done. It knows the game is up and will try anything to resist. There are many hooks to get attached to: altered states, fears, stories, stories about old stories, the past and the future.

There is a profound difference between living from our mind-centred idea of ourselves and living from our heart. We feel it differently in our being. This is what it means to surrender. It is not submission, it is to allow that way of being to come in more and more. Imagine living so fully that the mind was in service to the heart and could even drop away so that you just really lived from your heart alone, the higher mind just playing along to serve the deeper part of you, and helping in its expression.

What if you made the leap?

For yourself. For good. For ever. For humanity.

One day we will all make a great leap.

## STILL HERE

Come my love and stay a while
Hold me with your eyes and smile
When it's time for you to go
You'll still be here this much I know

Time with those we love is a beautiful treasure. We often don't give ourselves to those people and others as deeply as we could. Easily distracted by the day-to-day of life, we can find ourselves caught up in the trivial and unimportant.

Life lived deeply can be in connection with all the things we need to do, but also not wasted on things that draw us away, and are not supportive of our greatest health and highest good.

Eventually we run into questions of death and what remains. From the physical body and even the little deaths of small partings, the constant rise and fall of our experience. We have within us elements of everything that has gone before – our ancestors, the Earth, our individual and collective experiences.

The memories we have can be beautiful reminders, but they are all the sweeter when they are of times lived fully and with love. Meeting all changes with great love is transformative.

Our legacy is what we leave behind – for others, for future generations, for humanity. What if it was love, and the continuous inspiration to encourage love and unity in all beings? It is possible. Look at our great leaders, teachers, sages, artists and poets. They live on in the collective and they point us to the eternal both within and beyond us.

We are
all still
here.

## LOVE NEVER FAILS

If you could stop and see it all
Holding love amidst death's thrall
Knowing every fade to night
Is simply shade to morning's light
Nothing taken, nothing gone
A gentle closing of light well-shone
A passing time, an ocean crossed
Love never fails, is never lost

A life well-lived is full of love. For ourselves and others.

One of the big questions of life is, 'Do I love well?'.

I try. I've failed frequently and I keep trying. Towards myself and others. It is a continuing practice.

It can be a relief to know that whether you believe in reincarnation, a transmigratory essence, or the existence of a soul or not, that a life well-lived with love is beautiful and the true purpose of life itself. Our greatest acts live on in the hearts of others. They influence those close to us, the collective and the future of humanity.

We all know deeply that we are part of something much greater than ourselves or our ideas. As much as we get attached to many thoughts, emotions and material things, they are not all that we are.

The ultimate love into which we fall back is unfailing.

We may cross an ocean but we are still the ocean.

Love is the ocean.

## DISAPPEARED

Disappeared for I am gone
Music stops the dance goes on

We come to the end of this one divine song, but know that nothing truly ends. The greater dance of the divine is a continuation, just as we continue and are a continuation of each other.

What is it to disappear? A sense of 'I' completely gone?

All forms come and go.

There is no end to the dance.

Infinite Love.

## TIME IS TRUE

The time that time itself forgot
holds what is and what is not
The time that keeps the time is true
And does not pass its time is you

## ONE IN ALL

I will not rest until we all
find love in one and one in all

## BEACONS

Beacons lie along the road to gently guide the way
They shine so bright but go unseen as sun lights up the day
Don't gaze too hard, don't get too close, don't fly into the sun
They are there to guide you as your soul it journeys on

They gently point along the path your soul is here to take
Potential lies inside of you, your life is to awake
Sometimes they're a cloudburst, a lightning storm of rain
Sometimes they're the morning sun to lift you up again

Watch and listen carefully and venture down the path
The one that your soul chose to take is still the only truth
The signs are pointing every day so don't delay and start
The path of soul is always clear, just listen to your heart

The road will take you home again to what you always were
Every step in presence will take you back to here
Deeper back into yourself the quest is finally done
What you left in search of was to know yourself as one

All the loving power that dwells within your soul
Your intimate connection is here as you grow old
Give yourself to others but firstly to yourself
Beacons light the journey home for all of those who love

Those who love will lead us on to what we really are
Peace and understanding, our rising, guiding stars
A new Earth waits for all of us, to live in unity
Loving-kindness, wisdom, grace – a new humanity

## ACKNOWLEDGEMENTS

With much love and deep gratitude to these wonderful souls.
Your love, wisdom and kindness have touched my heart and
supported me in the most beautiful and important ways.

Ajahn Brahm, Andrea Walters, Br. Phap Dung, Debbie Ewington,
Jos Morrish, Julia Routley, Julie Edwards, Justine Buckley,
Kathryn Choules, Mark Probert, Michael 'Doko' Hatchett,
Morten Boe, Paie Haagsma, Ruth Gourley, Suzy Cooper,
Thich Nhat Hanh and especially to Makita Gabriel.

Also to the Noble Community at Plum Village in France, the
beautiful people at Soul Vida Fit, the Mudita Institute and
Byron Yoga Centre in Australia, and to my friends and family.

I hope you have seen yourself in these words. You are there.

I am also very grateful for the diligent work and expertise of
Aimée Longos, Josie Ferguson and Liam Relph. Their talents
in editing, proofreading and book design respectively have all
helped to bring my words to life and out into the world.

## ABOUT THE AUTHOR

Mark Simpson is an inspirational speaker and writer committed to raising personal and collective consciousness. Originally qualifying and practicing as a lawyer, Mark is now a yoga and meditation teacher who encourages transformation, healing and awareness. His work invites and supports individual and organisational growth and visionary leadership that is based on compassion, kindness, empowerment and inclusiveness.

He is the author of an accompanying collection of poetry entitled *Waking World* which is soon to be published, and a forthcoming work on the integration and embodiment of heart-based leadership and applied wisdom.

He lives in Perth, Western Australia.

For more information visit www.marksimpsonbooks.com